HALFWAY ACROSS THE RIVER

A story for the soul —

Annette Childs

Praise for *Halfway Across the River* and Annette Childs

"Annette Childs is a warm, bright, and accomplished psychotherapist who has spent the bulk of her career working with the dying and the bereaved, thus her writing comes from a heartfelt understanding of the struggles that eventually plague us all."

Raymond A. Moody, Jr., M.D., Ph.D.
Bestselling Author of *Life After Life*

"Annette Childs, artist of metaphors, has written another touching and meaningful book. *Halfway Across the River* offers lessons about life, death, grief, and transcendence. Although educational and enlightening, it is terrifically entertaining and reader friendly."

Dianne Arcangel
Author of *Afterlife Encounters and Life After Loss*

"For those of us who have spent our lives in the care of the dying, one of the greatest rewards come from those who share stories of moments that transcend the ordinary experiences of life. These moments arrive in the form of 'messages' from across the veil. Those who have the gift of recognizing these messages are charged with a great responsibility in sharing them with the rest of us. Dr. Annette Childs is one of these extraordinary individuals. In *Halfway Across the River* she has captured these stories with incredible grace, wisdom and compassion. Her latest book provides a message of hope for any who question, "Is this all there is?" Her stories help others to suspend their disbelief and provide hope for anyone who has experienced a loss."

Deb Girard RN
Founder, Circle of Life Hospice

Annette Childs, Ph.D. has been blessed with a natural ability to connect with invisible energies, enabling her to assist the dying and their loved ones as they cope with the process of transition. With humor and poignant honesty she has compiled dramatic examples of communication between this reality and the other side that will touch the heart of all who read it. *Halfway Across the River* is a beautiful and well written inspirational journey of peacefulness and love. This book will illicit spontaneous tears of joy, as fear is magically transmuted to a deep and reassuring understanding of the continuum that is life and death.

Jeffrey D. Millman, M.D.
Author of *A Giant Leap of Faith*

Accolades for Annette Childs and *Will You Dance?*

This debut work by Annette Childs received critical acclaim, and was named Gift Book of the Year and New Age book of the Year 2002.

A book for the journey...A story for the Soul

"Annette Childs has done the world a service by writing this book..."

Dr. Raymond A. Moody
Bestselling author of *Life After Life*

"Upon meeting Annette some years back, I was immediately overcome with the sense that this woman had a message to share with the world. *Will You Dance?* speaks to the wisest part within each of us, and this book will be a cherished companion for anyone traversing the dark night of the soul."

Andy Lakey
Author of *Art Angels and Miracles*

"What a beautiful, beautiful gift is being given to all through the publication of this book! A beam to show the reasons why and wherefore. This is a book for Little Ones and Old Ones and the heart in all of us who longs to know..."

Kanta Masters, President
Source Seminars

Will You Dance? asks us to face life's greatest challenge; to find the gift in whatever pain we encounter on our path through life. The book provides a profound and inspirational message to anyone facing change, loss and fear. Remarkably beautiful in prose and artistry, *Will You Dance?* makes a beautiful gift for those facing challenges in life. There is no one I can imagine that would not be touched by Dr. Childs' words of wisdom.

Wendy Oliver-Pyatt, MD Psychiatrist, and author:
Fed Up! The Breakthrough Ten Step No-Diet Fitness Plan

Will You Dance? is a symbolic story that defines the life experiences of most of us at one time or another. This is a highly recommended and enjoyable read, written in an almost poetic style."

Harold McFarland
Midwest Book Review
Amazon.com Top 50 Reviewer

"This is a book that feels right in your hands...a book to be read with the soul, not the brain."

Gloria Illene Madrigal
Author of *The Tree of Silence*

HALFWAY ACROSS THE RIVER

Messages
of hope
from
the
other
side

ANNETTE CHILDS, Ph.D.

HALFWAY ACROSS THE RIVER
Messages of hope from the other side
Annette Childs, Ph.D.

ISBN: 0-9718902-1-8 hardcover
ISBN: 0-9718902-2-6 paperback
Library of Congress Control Number: 2007937381

The Wandering Feather Press

774 Mays Blvd. #10-488
Incline Village, NV 89451

~FIRST PRINTING~

10   9   8   7   6   5   4   3

Editorial assistance: Pam Bickell
Cover design by Cyndee Bogard
Cover photography by Michael Imus
Book design and prepress by Paul Cirac

THE
Wandering
Feather
PRESS

Author's Note

This is the real story of events that transpired between Margaret Borwhat, Don Borwhat and myself. Unrelated stories about other people included herein are also true, but names and circumstances have been changed to ensure confidentiality. Aside from identifying details, the essence and content of the events are factual and describe real life occurrences.

Some of these stories may rub uncomfortably against your rational mind. To this, I say that irritation is necessary, for the smooth swell of a pearl is formed only to relieve the abrasion of an offending piece of sand.

If you find that these stories feel rough against the soft skin of your belief, sit with them a while and form your own pearl of truth around them. In this way, the pearl of great price is always your very own.

Dedicated to

Margaret
The wings that lift me

Brian
The arms that hold me

Sutter, Delaney, and Ajay
The lights that guide me

ACKNOWLEDGEMENTS

Don Borwhat. Without you, this book would still be sitting in my head. Yes, my friend, you bubble over with sarcasm, but you have a heart of gold, and I thank you for pushing me off the proverbial cliff so that I could fly.

To the patients and families who allowed me into their lives as they struggled to understand and cope with death and dying. There is no more intimate passage to share with another and I thank you for allowing me to be part of your journeys. Your place in my heart is deep and eternal.

To my parents, Bill and Grace. To say that I have walked to the beat of a different drummer would be a gross understatement. Thank you for always loving me, even when I know you could not understand me. You teach by example, and if I give half as much to others as you have given to me, then my life has been worthwhile.

And finally, to my husband Brian. I absolutely know that this book could not have arrived during any other time in my life. When I met you, my faith in the things of this world had grown dim. All that changed as I was enveloped in the simple goodness of your ways. It takes a rare man to love one who is so deeply called toward the invisible; not only do you tolerate my mystical nature, you celebrate it. Thank you. You have given me the ability to bring my best self forward to help others, and it is with you by my side that I have become who I always hoped I might be. Each day that we are together is the best day of my life, and I love you more than words can say.

CONTENTS

PART TWO

PART THREE

PART FOUR

AFTERWORD

THE LAST WORD 195

RESOURCES

PRELUDE

FOREWORD

Working in the field of death and dying, I have often been struck by the way death makes us want to turn the departed into heroes. Often it seems that our flaws die with us, and what is left to memory are the best parts of who we were. It seems ironic that the grace we do not offer to one another in our day-to-day living is somehow grandfathered in when we take our last breath.

This book tells the stories of individuals who have walked their last mile in this life. They are all people I have known. Some of them were lovely; others cantankerous, but all of them were extraordinarily ordinary. And though they were ordinary, in their dying they were able to touch the extraordinary, and that is why their stories are here for you to read.

Let me correct myself. The people in this book

were all ordinary except for one. Her name was Margaret Borwhat and she died an ordinary death but lived a truly extraordinary life. She was my dear friend and in her passing she somehow bequeathed me with the unenviable task of giving spiritual tutelage to her skeptical and rather difficult husband, Don.

Shortly after Margaret's death Don came to me with a story. He was like a teenager dropping off his term paper on the last day of school, trying to hand it off quickly so that he could move on to summer vacation. As you will see, I had to insist that Don stay after school for a bit, and finally enroll in summer classes as well. This book is really no more than me giving patient attention to Don while the uncanny spiritual events shared here, unfolded in his life. These events turned Don's previous worldview upside down, and together we sought a way for him to find balance. Indeed, if I was the tutor, and Don was the student, it was Margaret who was the real teacher to both of us.

Margaret left something behind for Don and I, which is truly a treasure without comparison. As you read her tale, you will come to know it as the white-rock story, and you may find yourself disbelieving my words. I cannot condemn your skepticism, for I have no answers as to how Margaret was able to pull off the spiritual shenanigan that she did. What I can tell you is that it really did happen, just the way I tell it.

Margaret entrusted Don and I with a beautiful sacred story, a true life occurrence that will open your heart and soul if you let it. It has taken courage for us to come forward with this story; it will take faith for you to read it.

If I had to guess at what allowed the cosmos to cooperate with Margaret Borwhat on the day the white-rock story unfolded, I would have to say I think it was simply the sum of her life. Margaret was a true master at performing small acts with great love, and if the worth of our good deeds is cumulative, she certainly had a spiritual bankroll that gave her carte blanche access to whatever she may have desired. What is so beautiful about Margaret is that I do not need to try and make her a hero through her death. Instead I can just tell you a few stories about her life, and you'll get it. I know you'll get it.

A House Blessing

A few months after Margaret's death, Don received an unexpected knock at the door. He opened it to find two Native American women dressed in the full regalia of their tribe. He began to shut the door as he told them he "did not want any," when the elder of the two spoke up in an authoritative tone.

"We are here to honor the life of Margaret Borwhat." Don inched the door back open and poked his nose through the opening.

"Excuse me?" he said, feeling a bit sheepish at his hasty attempt at closure.

"We are here to honor the life of Margaret Borwhat." Don had absolutely no idea what these two women were talking about, but of course when it came to anything having to do with his beloved Margaret, he was all ears.

Don invited them in and without hesitation they began to retrieve objects from a satchel one of the women carried over her arm. Don watched with bated breath as out came strange item after strange item: an abalone shell, a bundle of grass tied with string, and a few other odd things that Don could not identify.

At this point, even though these women had said the magic word "Margaret," Don felt he needed to put a halt to whatever game they were running. As he began his verbal request for them to cease and desist, he was struck by the way his words made the smaller of the two women recoil. She looked up at him, her eyes large and pleading.

"We only want to bless your home. It is our way of saying thank you to Margaret for the way she brought blessings to our grandmothers." The other woman went on to explain to Don that several years earlier Margaret had paid a visit to their Indian reservation. She had gone as part of the outreach she did for her breast cancer advocacy work. As she taught these tribal women about breast health and self-exams, she saw that a group of the elders could not read the pamphlets and written reminders that were an imperative part of the program.

Several weeks after her visit a packet of flyers had mysteriously arrived at the reservation. The flyers had been redone, printed in their native tongue. Unbeknownst to Don, Margaret had taken it upon herself to have the pamphlets translated into the native language of the tribal elders. She had this special batch of literature printed at her own expense and she had sent them to the reservation with not so much as a signed note to identify her good deed. That was Margaret: dying herself of breast cancer, yet filling her days with quiet acts of kindness that just might prevent someone else from having to walk in her unfortunate footsteps.

Don felt himself begin to sway side-to-side as the force that was Margaret's innate kindness crashed against him like a wave. He faltered backwards a bit to rest against the entry table as the women resumed their solemn unpacking. Before long the two were walking through his home with a trail of smoke following behind them, native prayers falling from their lips. Don watched in silent reverence. Although he did not exactly know what it was they were doing, he could feel the power of the moment. The goodness of it all was palpable.

He stayed put, leaning against the entry table. He was afraid he might not find his footing if he tried to walk. After a while, the two women came back to the entryway. They returned the sacred objects to the bag from where they had come. It was the elder that eventually spoke. "Your wife had a good and generous spirit. Your home will now be blessed because of her."

With that the two women left as quietly as they had come and Don was left standing alone in the shadow of Margaret's looming kindness.

For many weeks Don kept this story to himself. Perhaps this was in part because he did not know what to say or how to explain the enormity of it for him. Though he did not speak of it, the event replayed over and over in his mind. He wondered what other silent acts of kindness Margaret had carried out unobserved. It was not long before he got another small answer to his query.

Rx for the Soul

Don was enjoying a lazy, albeit lonely, Sunday morning perusing The Wall Street Journal, when he was roused by an unexpected knock at the door. He opened it to find a Hispanic gentleman with a whole gaggle of children standing behind him. The man spoke only broken English, and as best Don could tell, he was looking for Margaret and mentioning what sounded like yard work. Don thought perhaps this man was a day laborer who Margaret had employed in the past to help with their outdoor tasks. Don was courteous but firm. Margaret was not here and no he was not in need of any help at this time.

The man excitedly motioned to an old pickup truck in the driveway that sat heavy with rolls of fresh sod piled in its bed. Again Don was firm and politely motioned toward his fully landscaped yard, shaking his head "no" all the while. It was at this point one of the man's older children stepped forward. Removing his baseball cap in what seemed to be a gesture of respect, he quietly began to tell Don that this was not the first time that his father, Juan, had been to this house.

The previous summer Juan had been traveling the neighborhood looking for work, hoping to make extra money to pay for medications. When Juan had knocked those many months ago, it was Margaret who had answered the door. When she learned that Juan's wife was being treated for breast cancer and that the family could not afford the nausea medications that made the treatment bearable, her heart opened wide. She had motioned to a yellow patch of grass in the front yard, asking if Juan could replace her ailing grass for a fee. He sadly declined, and in his broken tongue he conveyed to her that he did not have the tools or the supplies to carry out this task.

Margaret was undaunted. She got in her car and followed his dilapidated pickup truck down to the nearest pharmacy where she paid cash to have every prescription that Juan had with him filled. Juan had never forgotten this kindness and the first signs of spring had found him at the local sod farm, filling his truck with what he hoped would be a fitting thank you to Margaret.

Don was speechless. Juan did not know Margaret's fate. Oh how he hated having to form the words, "Margaret has died." In this particular instance, the words carried such an echo, for he knew this family lived with the same thief that had taken Margaret. As Don delivered the news, the young man winced. His father seeing his expression needed no translation, and he immediately began to shake his head in sadness. Father and son spoke low to one another for a few moments, saying something that Don could not understand. The boy then looked at Don and said, "Please take this sod. It is a sign of our respect for your wife. It is all we have to offer you."

Don could do nothing other than bow his head in agreement. With this, Juan and his children began to unload the truck. Moving together like a well-oiled machine, they quickly piled the sod in neat even rows. When it was done, it somehow seemed like the most elegant floral arrangement Margaret could ever have been given.

As the pickup truck rattled away, Don took a deep breath and sat down on the front steps to survey the odd tribute that lay stacked in piles on the driveway before him. As he turned to go inside he knew who he had to call. "The Godwoman is gonna eat this stuff up," he said aloud—as he wiped the tears from his eyes.

• • •

Both of these events happened within months of Margaret's passing. She may be gone in body, but her strong spirit and innumerable acts of kindness continue to live on. These stories are just two of many that exemplify the life of Margaret Borwhat. She really was a master of carrying out small acts with great love. She had lived her life like a comet, traveling fast and burning bright. As you'll see in the pages of this book, Don and I would be chasing the tail of that comet together for many months, following her trail of light so that the pathway might be better lit for the rest of us.

PART ONE

WINTER COAT

Margaret Borwhat introduced herself to me with a phone call saying that she had seen an interview of me on television the night before, and that I was someone she absolutely had to meet. She explained that she had been having a particularly fear-filled and restless night and that in the wee hours of the morning she turned on the television for distraction, and there I was. She said she considered me to be her personal angel that night, offering the exact words she needed to hear, exactly when she needed to hear them. An ardent believer in the power of fate, I quickly put her on the books for my next available appointment.

As I waited for her to arrive for her appointment I wondered what this meeting would bring. In my many years of working with the dying I had become accustomed to serendipitous events and I looked forward to what would unfold with Margaret. As I sat at my desk doing paperwork, I glanced out the window just in time to see Margaret pull into the parking lot. As she got out of her car I was a bit surprised at what I saw, or perhaps it was what I could not see. I saw what looked like a very large, long, down-filled coat moving across the parking lot. Of course Margaret was inside the coat, but trust me, the coat was far larger than she was. And although it was a crisp autumn morning, the weather certainly did not warrant her wardrobe choice.

I smiled to myself as I watched this giant coat with legs move across the parking lot, touched by what I intuited from this vision. Margaret's cloistered wardrobe told me that she was not yet sure she wanted to reveal herself to me, a stranger who had spoken to her so eloquently through the television the week before. I had no doubt that on the morning she had called to schedule an appointment, she was acting on the strong conviction she had felt immediately after her uncanny middle of the night introduction to me. But as is often the case, convictions of the spirit can start to weaken under the weight of everyday life, and what seemed magical a week ago likely felt odd and maybe even a little crazy to her on that day. I was grateful she had kept her appointment with me.

I welcomed Margaret warmly into my office. Of course I asked if I could take her coat, to which she predictably said no. As she and her large coat sat down, I was struck by the sparkle in her eye. As we moved through the necessary jargon of a first meeting, I quickly began to hear the voice of a woman who was nothing less than mesmerizing to me, from the first words she spoke.

Margaret explained that she was a 15-year survivor of breast cancer. Since her diagnosis she had become one of the most notable breast cancer advocates in the United States, even speaking before Congress and successfully lobbying to have new treatments for this disease approved. She had recently been diagnosed with a recurrence of her cancer that she knew would result in her death. By her estimation she had a lifespan of no longer than three years. She was a realist if she was anything at all.

On the night she had seen my interview she had awoken from a fitful sleep, full of fear. Her fear was simple. She knew she was going to die, and she wanted to die well. She had spent the last fifteen years living well with a difficult disease. She realized her focus had to change. Now she needed to learn how to die well, but she had no idea where to turn to begin this new learning process. Unable to quiet her thoughts, she had turned on the television and to her astonishment there was an interview about dying well. It was at that moment the hand of fate began weaving the threads of our lives together.

NEW OLD FRIENDS

At our first meeting, Margaret settled onto the couch and at my urging, began to share a narrative of her life with me. Even though she was still hiding behind her big coat, within the first half-hour of conversation, I could see far enough into this woman to know that she was not meant to be a patient of mine. As a therapist who had been honing my skills with the dying for years, I could see that Margaret was a teacher like none I had ever met. She had sought me out because I had wisdom she needed. Yet as I listened to her speak, I realized she had an equal amount of wisdom to offer which I could use to better serve others.

When we came together that first day, it was a meeting of equals and I was immediately aware of this. Without hesitation, I announced to Margaret that I was sorry that I could not accept her as a patient of mine. Before her disappointment had time to set in, I smiled and explained to her that I would much rather be friends…friends on the same journey of making life better for cancer patients through our mutual desire to share wisdom and serve others. Both Margaret and I felt gentle unseen hands pushing us together that first day, and although neither of us could guess at where our friendship might lead, we were happy to be making the journey together.

PART ONE

COMMON GROUND

Margaret's big coat came off...both literally and symbolically. As she revealed herself to me in the weeks and months that followed our first meeting, I was introduced to one of the wisest, most grace-filled women I had ever met. She would later tell me that she had great reservations about coming to my office that first day, afraid that I was going to open up Pandora's Box and unleash all of the death related fears that she had kept at bay.

As the depth and connection between us grew, she often recounted to me the immense peace that she felt leaving my office that first day; a peace that she swore she was able to build upon each time we were together. I, too, felt peaceful and incredibly inspired in Margaret's presence. We both felt that we had great work to do together and we began honing our many visits around deciphering what it was that we could do together to assist the terminally ill in both living and in dying.

One thing was for certain. Both Margaret and I had a story to tell. Her story was one of triumph over her disease. She had truly mastered the art of living fully with a deadly disease. Her stumbling blocks became stepping stones for others. She was a way-shower and a leader, and in this role she truly flourished. She was a committed and tireless advocate for cancer patients and she truly made a difference in the lives of thousands. Her work can be witnessed through the women's advocacy network that she created, as well as through the workings of the charity Margaret's House *(www.wcan.org)* which is named in her honor.

My story was one of a different sort. I was a woman who had somehow been walking between worlds for most of my life. At a very young age I began to have uncanny experiences related to the dying which both enthralled and confused me. I was raised by conventional parents who found my esoteric interests to be somewhat unnerving. In hindsight it is apparent to all of us that my spiritual leanings were bubbling up not from my environment, but instead from an inner spring that lived within me.

The Catholic faith I was raised to believe in was simply too narrow for my expanding questions and by my early teens I had begun to explore all different forms of spiritual teachings. It was the tireless seeker within me that most interested Margaret, and just as she shared her inner self with me, I began to share with her some of the magic that had been part of my journey.

As a woman who has devoted her life to working with those at the end of life, I have had more than my share of unexplainable, "otherworld" experiences. I sometimes recount these experiences for my dying clients, and they are often soothed at hearing tales that hint at a greater reality after physical life has ended.

SHOW AND TELL

Margaret was no different in this way, and I shared many of my more memorable stories with her. She listened to these stories with a wide open heart and drank them in like a thirsty traveler. Although her faith was strong and she was a believer in the invisible realms, she was also very discerning. A wide-eyed neophyte who trusted blindly she was not! When I shared my stories with her, she pushed for details and engaged me in long conversations about possible ways to explain whatever phenomenon we were talking about. I loved this about Margaret. As a researcher myself, I shared her need to search for facts and hard evidence in the face of the great mystery of life and death.

Her trust in me and my love for her were pretty well complete when I made the decision to share the one story that had truly and forever altered my life and my relationship with reality. It was an occurrence I had not shared with many, because it is too unbelievable for most people to fathom. However, on the few occasions I had shared it with one of my dying clients I was always overwhelmed with the sense of peace and comfort it imparted.

I shared this story with Margaret and she was deeply moved. She felt so comforted and reassured by the events I related to her, that she began insisting that I absolutely had to find a way to get this story out to others. I brushed off her urgings for many weeks until finally one day quite earnestly she looked me right in the eye and said, "Annette, you must let this story be told; it is clearly something you are meant to do. I am dying and this story brings me such a sense of peace and belief in a larger reality. This story is an opportunity for you to bring a sense of comfort to thousands just like me."

I explained to her that I had tried on many occasions to find a way to share these extraordinary events, but I had a strong desire not to misuse or commercialize something that felt so sacred to me. To this she quickly countered, "Do you really think God gave you a beautiful experience like this so that you could keep it to yourself?"

Her words hit a chord deep within me, and my desire to filter the sharing of this experience suddenly felt selfish rather than honorable. It was true. I had been given a remarkable experience, one that I knew was too worthy to keep to myself. Together we began brainstorming ways to share the story with others. It was not long before Margaret suggested that we enlist the help of her husband and businessman, Don. I had briefly met Don a few times, but he seemed genuinely uninterested in the philosophical ramblings that took up the bulk of my visits with Margaret. He eyed me warily, and although he was always polite I could readily sense that he questioned my sanity.

Margaret described Don as her resident skeptic and confided in me that he had been sarcastically referring to me as "the Godwoman" for many months. She explained to me that he was a wonderful husband, a compassionate caregiver, and a very astute businessman, but that he still had many miles to travel when it came to believing in matters of the spirit.

She reasoned that Don's skepticism would be outweighed by the entrepreneur in him and decided that the three of us together—the skeptical businessman, the "Godwoman," and she who was dying of cancer—could find a way to share a story that she felt could make a positive difference in the lives of so many. And so there we were, three unlikely companions traveling together toward a destination that is still unfolding today.

DESTINATION UNKNOWN

The day of our first meeting was anxiety provoking for me to say the least. I knew Don thought I was odd, and I was not at all interested in converting him away from his narrow beliefs. Margaret had asked that I share with Don first hand the encounter that was the basis for our plans. I had decided that I was more comfortable writing the experience down for Don to read than I was telling him outright. I knew Don thought I was a few sandwiches shy of a whole picnic to begin with, and I did not have the gall to attempt a verbal rendition of my experience. I handed him my small stack of papers and sat back and waited for his response. Following is the actual narrative that I shared with Don that day.

THE STONE MADONNA

During the summer of 1998 my family and I took a vacation to Carmel, California. I had the opportunity to meet an artist named Andy Lakey. Andy is well known for a specific type of angel artwork that I had been collecting. He was familiar with my work with the dying and had agreed to meet me shortly before his public art show that night.

I waited quietly in the gallery anticipating Andy's arrival. Before long the door opened and I found myself face to face with Andy. A combination of intensity and warmth, we spoke easily, as if we had been in comfortable conversation together many times before. As our conversation ensued, Andy suddenly became pensive. He placed his hands on my shoulders and looked as much at me as through me and he spoke these words, "You came into this life to write. You came to teach and to tell the story that your soul knows." He was very intent as he said this, to the point that I looked away and stammered a bit.

He said it one more time, holding my gaze, and then quietly excused himself. Although these words may sound benign, at that moment they hit me like an avalanche. His words caused something deep within me to stir. The rest of the evening carried on without reference to what he said, but I felt strangely altered by our conversation. Rather than feeling excited, I began immediately to feel a sense of trepidation. There was an instant recognition within me of the great responsibility taken on when choosing to "tell one's story." The silent doubts quickly swept in, and I felt I had taken a step forward into a world that seemed unfamiliar and completely beyond my control.

The next morning, we awoke to a beautiful coastal day. Never having been to Carmel before, I decided to take the kids to the stunning white sand beaches. My sleep the night before had been fitful and my mood was somber. My spirits lifted as the beach came into view. At first walking and then beginning to run, we tumbled head on toward the beach. The kids were laughing as they struggled to stay upright running down the steep decline that led to the water.

As we walked along the beach, the relentless pounding of the surf and the cool salt water breeze made a natural backdrop for a deep sense of reverence. As the kids ran before me darting in and out of the small waves that lapped at the shoreline, I silently began to pray. I had been as equally touched as disturbed by the words Andy Lakey had spoken to me the evening before. If, indeed, I did have a sacred calling that involved writing books, I felt incredibly unsure of how to even begin the process. One look at the beaming faces of my two children in the shallow surf told me that my moment of quiet reflection was likely to be short lived. Wasting no time at all, I closed my eyes and sent out a sincere invocation to the universe. My request was simple: If my writing was indeed a way to heal the lives of many, then I needed a sign.

With that I released my worries to the cosmos, ended my moment of reverence and went to join my children on their walk down the beach. The heaviness I had felt since meeting Andy was replaced by a deep sense that this situation now lay in higher hands. Although writing had always been my dream, it was a dream I had thus far been unable to manifest in my life. I felt liberated, liberated from Andy's expectations and, in a sense, freed from my own hopes and dreams about writing a book.

The kids began running slightly ahead of me. As I

walked along in the surf, enjoying the interplay of reced-
ing sand and surf beneath my feet, a small stone that had
been tumbling recklessly back toward the ocean, suddenly
anchored itself at my feet. Although there was no sound, a
tangible force held the stone still as the rushing water
receded around it.

As my eyes began to assimilate this form it was as if the
waves had stopped. I stared in stunned silence at what lay
beckoning at my feet. I knelt down and with shaking hands
picked up what I have now come to call the stone Madonna.
The significance of this small stone which lay in the palm of
my hand cannot readily be conveyed in words. It was an
exact replica of the central figure on my meditation altar at
home.

I turned the small icon over in my hands and was utter-
ly speechless at the detail of this gift from the sea. My
daughter came to see what it was that so gripped my atten-
tion. In wide-eyed wonder she squealed that this was "the
mommy and baby lady" that I loved so much. Her deep blue
eyes looked at me approvingly and she scampered off to find
a treasure of her own.

I stood up, my eyes shifting from the clear blue sky to the
outstretched horizon of the sea, to the small figure in my
still shaking hands. A visual trinity was forming around me
as I stood in the surf, white foam mandalas swirling around
my ankles. As I turned to walk back to my children, nothing
was as it had been. I began to walk a path that moment
which to this day continues to unfold.

Upon returning home, I remained in a deep sense of reverence, literally seeing the world through eyes that had been enlivened by some inner force. I made my way through those first few days somewhat superficially, still feeling the quiet hum of divine contact within me. Five or six days after returning home, I went to our local grocery store to retrieve our vacation photographs. As I finished my grocery shopping, I absentmindedly reached into my purse to peruse our photographs. I was wholly unprepared for what was waiting for me.

The first dozen pictures were vintage family vacation shots. I smiled as I relived our outings in Carmel. In the middle of this envelope of vacation photos was a picture taken on the beach the day the stone Madonna appeared. My hands began to tremble. In front of me was a picture of myself and the kids, ocean waves in the background. The sky was a beautiful azure blue, and above us are dozens of opalescent balls of light. They looked like small orbs descending upon us.

The scene was breathtaking in its sheer beauty. It had been snapped just a few minutes after the stone had washed onto the shore before me and as I looked down at this picture, I was overcome with the grace I had been given. Leave it to me to have one of the most profound moments of my life while standing in the middle of a grocery store. The universe has nothing if not a sense of humor.

I began to look around the store now, feeling a sense of urgency, trying desperately to get my bearings. As I stood in the middle of that busy supermarket, unbeknownst to anyone else, my world was shifting around me. I had the unmistakable sensation that my feet now lay on a distinct path and that I was urgently being guided to follow.

It is said that when our calling arrives, the whole universe becomes very, very still, as if our guardian angels hold their breath, waiting to see if we can hear the still small voice that tells us who we are. On this day that inner voice was not so still and not so quiet. As I left the supermarket I walked out the door into a brand new world. I closed my eyes and took a deep breath. I agreed to answer the call.*

Don read my narrative and without saying a word he promptly laid the typed pages down before him. He briefly scanned the photograph and stone Madonna that I had ceremonially laid out on the table while he was reading. When he looked up at me his expression was a mixture of pity and humor. He turned to Margaret with a look of exasperation and promptly announced that he did not think he was the right one to help us in our quest to share this story with others.

Margaret quickly admonished him to "just get over it" (referring to his skepticism) and turned her attention back to me and the matter at hand. Like a vehicle traveling with one flat tire, the three of us

* *to read more about this occurrence and to see the actual photograph visit www.onecandle.net.*

began the bumpy task of trying to move forward together on this project.

It was clear from the outset that the businessman and the Godwoman had little in common. My mystical yearnings were much too "foo foo" for a man of Don's logic, and his hard nosed business skills were quite distasteful to my idealistic vision. In spite of our differences, we committed ourselves to working together as a team. The one thing we did share was a love and respect for Margaret.

SPIRITUAL BOARD ROOM

Over the next six months, try as we may, the skeptical businessman, the Godwoman, and the woman dying of cancer, could not bring our talents together in a way that allowed us any progress. We would meet, Don with his poster board ready to make flow charts to map out our goals. The charts remained empty, but the air was always full of a great sense of expectancy. The three of us would end up deep in conversation that was rich and meaningful but at the end of each day, our goal remained unmet.

What did happen, though, was that Don's respect for me began to increase, my aversion to selling "my story" diminished, and Margaret's cancer continued to grow. Margaret was still our referee, but she began ever so slightly to step aside, allowing a real kinship to form between Don and me. At this point, when he called me "the Godwoman" his sarcasm had been replaced with genuine warmth.

Don still thought I was nuts, but he now understood that my friendship with Margaret was sincere, and that crazy as it seemed to him, my stories and philosophies were giving her great comfort as she moved ever closer to the end of her life. In some strange way, the three of us were each taking our place in a cosmic puzzle that none of us yet had the vision to see.

SLOW MOTION

It was in the wee hours of an October morning that I heard the phone in my home office ring. As the answering machine picked up, I heard Don's distressed voice on the other end of the line. "Annette, this is Don. Margaret has taken a turn for the worse. We are at the hospital. The doctors are telling me she is dying. She asked me to call you." With this his voice trailed off, his sorrow palpable through the phone line. I immediately called him back and told him that I would be at the hospital within the next few hours.

As I got ready to leave for the hospital I became quite emotional at the prospect of losing my dear friend. Although Margaret's disease had been progressing, she was so lively and engaged in life it was easy to let myself forget she was dying. Before heading out the door to the hospital, I sat down and began to pray. I asked simply that I be an instrument of peace and healing to Margaret in her time of need.

Prompted by a strong inner urge I walked over to a glass china hutch in my foyer. In our home this hutch is an altar of sorts, and it is where I keep all of the things that are sacred to me. At the center of all the items in this hutch sits the stone Madonna and the photo from Carmel. These items have become a spiritual touch point for me and when I seek higher guidance they normally are a part of my prayer ritual. I briefly thought of bringing the stone Madonna with me to the hospital, but this thought was immediately replaced with the strong sense that Margaret should have her own stone to hold on to.

On the bottom shelf of the hutch sat a group of small heart-shaped rocks that I had collected through the years. I scanned them for a moment and picked two of them up, a white one for Margaret so pure of heart, and a blue one for Don, as I knew his heart was blue with sadness at this time. I slipped the stones into my pocket and headed out the door to see my ailing friend.

My walk down the corridor of the oncology unit toward Margaret's room was a solemn one. As I passed the many rooms filled with gaunt faces and bald heads it was a grim reminder of the incredible physical toll this disease takes on those diagnosed with it. As a tireless cancer patient advocate, Margaret had spent the last 15 years of her life working determinedly to make prevention, treatment and education available to people just like the ones in the hospital.

Unlikely as it sounds, I was caught off guard to realize that Margaret was not just their advocate. Today she was one of them, lying in a hospital bed, struggling to breathe with a plethora of beeping machinery playing its sad melody around her. As her room number came into view, everything began to move in slow motion. I could make out the silhouette of Margaret in her hospital bed. She looked so small and frail, and for the first time since I had known her, I could see the bald head that she always kept covered with either a wig or brightly colored scarf.

This hit me incredibly hard; during the two years of our friendship I had rarely seen Margaret look anything but vibrant. Although she sometimes wore the telltale turban of her disease, she always had such a strong physical presence it was easy to forget the war that raged beneath her skin.

I had to gather myself before walking into her

room, determined not to let my sudden abject sorrow show itself to my dear friend. As I entered the room Margaret was dozing quietly and Don stood to greet me. Our eyes met and our silence was heavy with knowing. He shook his head sadly from side to side telling me without words that the news the doctors were giving him about Margaret was not good. He left quietly then, wanting to allow Margaret and I a few moments alone together.

Margaret began to rouse and as she turned to look at me, I could see a slow smile appear beneath the oxygen re-breather that was strapped to her face. That was Margaret in a nutshell, pulling herself from the fog of her illness to bless me with her beautiful smile. I spoke gently to her and she was able to tell me how surprised she was that this was the end of her life. She, too, had been taken aback by the swiftness with which she had deteriorated.

As we talked, I dug into my pocket and brought out the white stone heart. As I placed it gently in the palm of her hand I leaned in and whispered to her, "Just as you hold this small stone in your hand, know that you too are held in the palm of a gentle hand unseen. You are never alone Margaret, I promise." She tightened her hand around the stone and her eyes filled with tears. I too began to cry softly. I promised her that I would be by her side through wherever these last days were to take her. She thanked me and

I turned to see that Don had come back into the room.

I stood up and reached into my pocket to retrieve the blue heart. As I handed it to him, he looked at the rock in his outstretched palm and looked up at me quizzically. He wore an expression of utter confusion as he moved his hand back toward me as if to say, "Nice rock, but you keep it." Before he could give it back, Margaret's voice floated up between the two of us. "Don, Annette is giving you a gift...take it." Don surrendered without much of a fight and mustered a weak thank you before quickly putting the stone in his pocket and out of sight.

The three of us laughed then, suddenly feeling once more like the odd trio that had begun the task of working together those many months ago. Once again we were like a car trying to travel with one flat tire, the skeptical businessman, the Godwoman, and the one dying of cancer. Only this time we knew our destination and we knew that three would soon become two.

As the days passed Margaret became less and less responsive. Don and I interacted a bit like two little kids being forced by their mothers to play with one another. We each stayed in our respective comfort zones, me doling out the spiritual comfort that Margaret craved, and Don attending to her every emotional, physical and social need. Don arranged for their son Chris and a variety of other relatives to fly in to be with Margaret.

As Margaret's condition weakened I spent less time at the hospital, not wanting to intrude on the precious time she had left with her immediate family. My last visit with Margaret had been unabashedly full of emotion for both of us. She pleaded with me to continue my work, and to write so that I could bring hope and comfort to others like her. When I said goodbye to Margaret that day I think we both knew that it would be our last meeting. I walked through a drizzling rain to my car and sobbed outright. I already missed Margaret. She had been such a grand friend to me, offering me wise council, sharing with me the unfiltered truth of what it was like to be terminally ill and hopeful that I would use her honesty to help others facing the same plight.

Most touching to me was the simple fact that Margaret trusted me to be her companion on this last journey. I was overcome with the desire to make her death count. Feeling the weight of responsibility bearing down on me, much like that day so many years ago in Carmel, I once again looked skyward and began to pray. "Please. Please show me the way."

PART ONE

KEEPING VIGIL

I never did see Margaret again. The rest of her days were difficult ones spent in the ICU with only her family at her side. I did send Don a few text messages rich in the language of metaphor that Margaret loved. He would reply back with short phrases like, "Huh?" and "I don't get what you mean." Rather than pepper Don with jargon that he did not have the energy to translate, I ceased with the "meaningful" text messages and resorted to the simple act of prayer on their behalf.

Unbeknownst to me at the time, the white rock that I had given Margaret became an important source of comfort to her. Don later told me that she held that rock in her hand continuously in those last days. When she would drift away to sleep and lose her grip on it, Don would quickly retrieve it from the bed sheets and hold it until she awoke again. The moment she opened her eyes, he would gently place it back into the palm of her hand. This gentle interplay happened repeatedly between them as she lay dying: Don held the stone for Margaret when she drifted away and when she was able to stay alert, Margaret held onto that stone just as she was holding onto her very life.

The day before Margaret died she was able to have

a highly coherent talk with Don. In this brief conversation she made two things very clear. The first was her desire that Don continue on with her work. She wanted him to carry the torch that she had lit for cancer patients everywhere. Don countered that he was a businessman and not a philanthropist. He could manage funds for a non-profit but he was not a people person like she was. To this, she simply repeated the mantra that she had lived her life exemplifying, "When you are asked to help, don't make excuses, just help."

The other thing Margaret told Don point blank was that she was going to leave behind a story that would make me finish my book. Don being the literal person he is was not sure what she was referring to, but because she was incredibly short of breath and it made speaking difficult, he quickly nodded his agreement. She then took the white rock and placed it in his hand telling him that he should hold the stone now; her peace was within her and it was he who would need to find solace. Don knew that she was saying goodbye with this gesture. He held onto the stone as Margaret drifted into an unconscious state from which she would not return.

During the final moments of Margaret's life, Don once again placed the stone in her hand. The interplay of passing this stone back and forth between them had become rich with meaning and he simply wanted to carry out the ritual one more time. He closed her hand around the stone and began the vigil of sitting beside his beloved mate on the last day of her life. Sometime after this Margaret's breathing became quiet and then gently stopped altogether. Her battle was over, and she lay quiet. The beeping machinery was turned off, and the medical staff left the room to give the family some time with Margaret to say good-bye.

When the final goodbyes had been said, Don gently opened Margaret's hand to retrieve the white heart shaped stone. Her hand was empty. Reasoning that the stone had slipped from her hand unnoticed in those last moments, Don began combing through the hospital bedding—yet it was nowhere to be found. He enlisted the help of the ICU staff in looking for it, but despite everyone's best efforts, Don left the hospital that day without the stone.

He was beside himself. Now the very thing that had been such a source of comfort to both he and Margaret in those last days was just one more painful loss. He kept reliving Margaret's request that he hold onto the stone, and he was filled with a sense of deep bereavement that this last connecting point between them was somehow gone. When he got home from the hospital he carefully went through the bag of Margaret's belongings. One by one he patted and shook every item that had accompanied her to the hospital. He looked through the pockets of every pair of pants he had. He checked his coats. He searched the overnight bag he had kept for himself, all to no avail.

Despite his laborious effort, the stone was simply gone. Don's sadness over this additional loss was a lonely grief, for no one besides Margaret knew anything about the way they had passed this stone between them during her last days. Even though I had given her the stone on her first day in the hospital, I had no idea that it had been so cherished, or that it had been lost.

PART TWO

A Stone's Throw from Heaven

In the week after Margaret's death, Don had the comfort of close family around him so we did not talk much. I knew that Margaret had wished to be buried in her home state of New York and Don was busy making arrangements to have her body flown back to the East Coast where her funeral would take place. I spoke to him before he left and he was getting through those first days by keeping his focus on the details of the tribute that would take place to honor Margaret's life.

Don took great care to make sure her funeral was an impeccable representation of an extraordinary life. The cards, flowers, and e-mails he had been receiving since Margaret's death truly exemplified the thousands of lives she had touched with her tireless efforts on behalf of others.

In some odd way, the pomp and circumstance of this final event was very healing, and on the eve of Margaret's funeral Don found himself feeling quite peaceful as he sat alone in his Amsterdam, New York hotel room. As he got ready to retire for the night, he carefully laid out the clothes he would wear in the morning and went over the list of last minute details he had to accomplish the next day. By the time he turned the lights out at 10:00 pm, everything was in its place and he anticipated waking to an uncomplicated morning.

Don did not rouse until the clock radio beeped its alarm the next morning. It was the first time he had slept the entire night since Margaret had died and he was both surprised and pleased. As he opened his eyes, he was still thick with the fog of a heavy sleep. He focused on the unfamiliar surroundings and for a moment he could not think of where he was.

Reality came swift and hard. He covered his face with his hands as he realized that today was the day he was going to bury the one he had loved since they were twelve years old...yes, Don and Margaret had been childhood sweethearts. He lay in bed for a moment wondering how he was going to get through the day. Out loud he said, "Margaret, how am I going to do this?" He turned his head toward the pillow where, if she were still with him, she would be laying.

His breath caught and he felt suddenly paralyzed

by what he saw. Next to him on the pillow was the white stone heart. He scrambled up and out of that bed as if it were on fire. He stood disbelieving and rubbed his eyes. Two or three times he repeated this action of rubbing his eyes and each time his blurred vision became clear, the rock was still on the pillow. Like an animal trying to distinguish between friend and foe, he circled the bed guardedly, finally bending down near the rock to look closer at it.

He was not sure he wanted to touch it. His mind raced. Was this some sort of cruel practical joke? Was someone somewhere laughing at the thought of his confusion? He looked around the room for signs that someone had entered during the still of the night. The room was just as he had left it the night before. His clothes for the funeral were still carefully laid out. His to-do list sat on the nightstand where he had left it before falling to sleep.

The silence in the hotel room was deafening as the logical, airtight world Don had constructed around himself for over 50 years came crashing down like breaking glass. Don sat and he began to shake; not the small tremors of a morning chill, but the full body shuddering that accompanies shock.

As he gathered his thoughts, he began to reconstruct the last weeks in his mind with as much detail as he could muster. He was certain he had told no one at all about the rock. Among his family and friends

Don was known as nothing if not a staunch rational-
ist. He knew that the only person he would have
talked to about the rock was me, and he had felt so
badly about losing it, he had purposely avoided the
conversation.

He sat very still in the chair, never taking his eyes
off the stone which lay in its own quiet glory on the
pillow across the room from him. Margaret had given
it back to him. He knew this in the way one knows
truth, the kind of truth that wraps itself completely
around your being and settles into your very bones.
As he sat there, anchored to the chair by the weight
of his own knowing, the long held beliefs that Don
had built his world around began to slip away, like
sand through an hourglass.

He was surprised at himself. If Don had ever
imagined what it might feel like to receive proof of
life after death, this wasn't it. Although agitation is
not quite the correct word, joy is equally as obtuse in
describing the emotion that now washed over him.
He felt as if he had been sitting in the chair for an
eternity, but when he glanced at the clock radio, he
was surprised to see that just a few minutes time had
lapsed.

A few minutes and an entire lifetime, he thought
to himself. He got up and walked over to the pillow,
and with a shaking hand he picked up the stone.
It was cool and smooth in his hand, and instantly

familiar. The memory of he and Margaret handing the stone back and forth brought back a flood of emotion as he remembered those last days in the hospital.

He closed his hand tightly around the stone and not knowing what else to do, he thanked Margaret out loud for this gift. As the stone warmed in his hand, the warmth began to radiate throughout his entire being. His state of confusion was burning off like morning fog, and a deep sense of peace was quieting his mind. He could feel true unadulterated joy rising in his heart. For that moment, he knew the truth. He knew that Margaret still existed in some form, and he knew that she was letting him know that wherever she was, all was well.

Standing on Bedrock

He began to dress for the funeral, feeling nothing like he had imagined he would the night before. His grief was still there and the hollow place in his world that Margaret once occupied was deep, but beneath his sadness was now a layer of knowing that was like bedrock beneath him.

Throughout the morning Don would, every few minutes, reach into his pocket to finger the stone. Each time, there was a surge of anxiety in the split second between his thought of the rock, and his ability to locate it in his pocket. The stone heart was such a treasure to him its safekeeping felt like an unbearable burden. What if he lost it? Just the thought of it made his stomach tight with worry, making him instantly aware of the grief that would ensue should he somehow misplace the rock.

So, at the final closing of Margaret's casket he knew what he wanted to do. For the last time, Don carried out the gentle ritual that had begun during those days in the hospital. The stone was still warm as he placed it gently into Margaret's hand. Don felt an odd sense of completion as he carried out this last gesture with his beloved wife. He knew he would carry the white stone heart within him forever, and that it was now secure in Margaret's safekeeping.

Throughout the funeral and the days spent with family and friends afterwards, Don said nothing to anyone about the stone. His sense of peace was continual, but his mental chatter was nearly relentless. Don had been raised Catholic, but really held no deep and abiding faith in an afterlife. Quite the opposite actually. He believed that once you died, that was it, end of story. Now he felt certain there was some type of afterlife, but he had absolutely no container in which to hold the flood of faith that had befallen him. Like a lottery winner with no access to a bank, Don felt like he had received this great windfall, yet had nowhere to put it.

His mind raced constantly. Just the general semantics of a true afterlife completely befuddled his logic. He wondered things like, How does an afterlife work? Where does it start? Is Margaret always with me, or does she just visit sometimes? How do I find my way to where she is when I die?

Foo Foo 411

As the days wore on, Don's relentless self talk began to chip away at his inner peace. Was he losing his mind? Did he imagine the white stone? Now that it was out of his sight, could he be sure it really had been on the hotel room pillow?

The first thing that Don did upon returning home was to call me. Seeing his name come up on my caller ID, I answered the phone with a warm hello, anxious to touch base since we had not talked in several weeks. Don's tone was warm but troubled. His sense of urgency was tangible. "Godwoman, I need to talk."

With just the slightest prompting on my part, Don poured out the incredible events of the last week. I listened in stunned silence, tears falling like rain. In all my years of work with the dying, I had heard special stories from the newly bereaved, but I had never heard one quite as beautiful as the story Don was sharing over the phone.

Perhaps most meaningful of all to me was the way Margaret had so beautifully and succinctly wiped away Don's staunch disbelief in an afterlife. As far as I could tell, she had been flawless in her delivery. If she had manifested the rock in any explainable way what-soever, Don would have quickly rationalized it away. I knew this as well as she did. Manifesting that stone in a hotel room nearly 3,000 miles from where it had gone missing was such a "Margaret" thing to do. She was always impeccable in her ways and a stickler about following through with her plans. As Don shared with me the conversation between them in which she vowed to leave me with a story that would allow me to finish my book, a quiet knowing began to hum like an engine within me.

Although I was tempted to throw myself into writing then and there, I first needed to help Don acclimate to this strange world he now lived in. Since he had returned home from New York, there had been a steady stream of unexplainable phenomenon occurring in his home. There had been nothing as grand as the white rock to be sure, but there were many small things that warranted Don's attention none the less.

Don't Forget to Smell the Coffee

One of the incidents occurred on the day Don had to make the decision to put Margaret's beloved dog to sleep. The dog, Emily, had been sick for years, and despite Don's devoted care, he knew it was time to end her suffering. He carried out the grim task with the trademark love and devotion Don gave to those he loved. He returned home to a quiet house and with a heavy heart he began to make a pot of coffee.

Out loud he said, "Margaret, I hope I did the right thing today." At that moment two things happened simultaneously. The first is that Don distinctly heard Margaret chiding him with a phrase that had been an inside joke between them for more than twenty years: "Don, don't forget to smell the coffee." Years ago when she had said it to him the first time, she meant for him to wake up to the obvious. It was her polite way of saying, "Duh!" to her husband.

So in Don's mind he heard Margaret's unique form of "Duh!" loud and clear, and at the same moment the light bulb in the ceiling directly above the coffee pot blew out with a loud pop. It startled Don enough that he jumped and spilled the coffee. As he bent to clean up the coffee, he could indeed smell it! He shook his head in laughter and disbelief. "Yes, Margaret, I can smell the coffee."

With that, the weight of his grief over Emily was washed away like a footprint in the surf. Over the next months when his cynical mind began to pipe up, Margaret would almost immediately quell its chatter with another event. He would call me, often exasperated at yet another strange happening that hinted at Margaret's continued presence in their home. His emotions about this ran the gamut from pleasant surprise to near frustration about the way his world seemed to be changing, beyond his control.

Despite the differences that once kept Don and I at a distance from one another, we were now becoming genuine friends. The irony of this was not lost on me. One of the things that I had spent so many long hours discussing with Margaret was the way that a high-level spiritual experience seemed to change people in ways that were truly life altering. She was very interested in this, and it was one of the things she really encouraged me to write about. It almost seemed as if she had sent me the ideal research candidate in Don.

In the few months since Margaret's death, Don had truly transformed in a myriad of ways, and much of the transformation was against his will! Don had done his best to remain the logical, aloof, businessman he had always been, but now one of the main topics of conversation between the two of us was his overwhelming desire to "give back." Although he was feeling a deep inner desire to become more philan-

thropic in his pursuits, he was also genuinely surprised and baffled at where this sudden charitable
nature was coming from.

He still called me the Godwoman and often
blamed me with mock anger for ruining his ability to
enjoy his cutthroat business deals using his former
"take no prisoners" way of thinking. It was not
uncommon for him to express to me his disapproval
of how pathetic he had become since having the mis-
fortune of meeting me and agreeing to Margaret's
hair-brained scheme that we should work together.
Of course, it gave me great pleasure to hear him
whine about these things, and so began our joint
efforts to make the world a better place.

Don and I now shared a sense of destiny.
Margaret had made it clear to me while she was alive
that the experiences I had shared with her had helped
to quell her fear of death. Her greatest desire was to
help me put these experiences into book form, so
that others facing her same struggles might find some
peace on their journey as well. Margaret left this
world telling Don she wanted him to use his skills to
help others and that she was going to do her best to
give me a story that would allow me to finish my
book. Her manifestation of the white rock succinctly
accomplished both of her dying goals. Now it was up

to Don and me to map out a means to tell our story in a way that helped others.

The one thing that Don and I definitely agreed upon was the power of a single event to turn one's world upside down. When the white stone heart turned up on the pillow in New York, Don's whole world changed. That day in Carmel when the stone Madonna washed up at my feet, my life too, was forever altered.

It was intriguing to both Don and I that it was the story of the stone Madonna that had brought Margaret so much comfort as she faced her own death, and then it was a stone that she had used as her calling card when she turned Don's cynical world upside down in New York. I e-mailed Don and told him that perhaps we should call our project "Stones from Heaven" and with typical Don Borwhat sensitivity, he fired off this reply to me:

> "The title could also be:
> *Hit in the head by a rock*
> *I forgot to duck*
> *Thick as a rock*
> *Dumb as a rock*
> *Beating sense into one with a rock*
>
> These would all describe Margaret's efforts to get me to open up to foo foo. No

matter what you write about me you're always
going to be the Godwoman cursed with a life
full of foo foo and forced to help others."

—*Don*

   And so it went as Don and I moved along our path
together. Before we could proceed very far, Don
needed first to begin to understand what had happened to his life. He had no choice but to accept the
unexplainable events that had befallen him in these
last months, yet he needed some type of framework
in which to contain his new world. Other than me,
Don did not know another living soul that he could
talk to about his experiences. He was more than a little disturbed at the notion that he and I were beginning to have some things in common.
   I will never forget the day he came to me in all
earnestness and asked, "Godwoman, were you born
this way or did you just wake up all foo foo one day?"
I would have laughed out loud had the look on his
face not been so serious and pleading. I tried to
answer Don's question in the same tone it had been
asked, but it was hard to be serious and use the word
foo foo at the same time.
   As I dissolved into laughter Don threw up his
hands and announced that I had single-handedly
"ruined his freakin' life and he just wanted to go back
to his old world of being a righteous SOB who got his

kicks in the boardroom." With that he got up and walked away. He managed a quick glance back at me and I could see the familiar grin that told me he would be calling me soon. And of course he did.

BUILDING A HOUSE OF TRUTH

I knew Don was struggling, really struggling, and there really was nothing funny about it. When your belief system fails to hold up beneath the weight of your life experiences, it creates a crisis of the spirit. It is something I have seen time and again among those who begin to have a true sense of how multi-dimensional reality can become. Don was on an emotional roller coaster, vacillating between incredible waves of peacefulness and moments where he worried that he was losing his mind.

I had felt these same things once; thus, I was enabled throughout my career to help many of my clients find balance within these same conflicting emotions. I have always told my clients "that it was up to them to build their own house of truth, a personal shelter for the beliefs that reflected their unique experience of reality." I had learned early in my journey that I did not want the responsibility of handing my beliefs down to anyone else; in other words I knew that my house of truth was home to me alone.

I knew I could not give Don the answers he was seeking, but I could share with him the things that were true for me in that moment. The first of these personal truths was that I simply lived my life in a state of expectancy. Each day I remained open to the miraculous, and more often than not the universe delivered. Most days found me sitting in gratitude for the small miracles that were meaningful to no one but me. Other days, like the one in Carmel, simply took my breath away.

I never knew what each new day would bring, but my perpetual state of expectancy seemed to keep the door to the miraculous open in my world. My journey was a quiet one, despite the fact that many of my days bore the watermark of another world. I preferred to think of myself as an everyday mystic and like an artist who has honed her craft, I had found a way to blend both the miraculous and the mundane flawlessly onto the canvas that was my life.

One thing I had learned was that individuals in the last stages of their lives seemed to have more access to other realms than did those who were busy with the tasks of living. To this Don quickly countered that when one is lying in bed dying, he has nothing better to do than let his imagination run wild. He had a point, and I acknowledged this. I told him the only proof I had to counter his thought was the myriad of experiences in my own life that said otherwise. But these experiences were really of no good to anyone but me.

My neutrality was frustrating to Don. It was as if he was treading water, and there I sat in the life boat chiding him to swim a little farther rather than throwing him a line. He pushed me for explanation: "Why after 50-plus years of being perfectly happy in my logical, agnostic world, am I finding myself trapped in this foo foo sh-t?"

Again I had to suppress a smile. His question was achingly serious to him. I gave Don a beautiful and succinct metaphor, and although it was wisdom that I certainly knew like the back of my hand, I had never couched it in these terms, and as I heard myself speaking the words, I was surprised at the profundity of the simple allegory that was moving through me.

I explained to Don that as people move toward the end of their lives, they begin to have access to more subtle levels of reality. They become like a watch that ticks faster than other watches around it. For those who are very close to or are caring for the departing, just to be sitting in the proximity of them causes the caregivers to begin ticking a bit faster themselves.

I added that I believed that being with someone at the moment of their death, particularly being in a state of peace rather than a state of fear, resulted in a permanent sort of 'speed up' in their ticking that gave them a bit more access to the subtle realms. Don's face lit up with instant recognition. He didn't say much, just that my explanation made a lot of sense to him, but the sense of relief he felt was evident. I was pleased that my metaphor had hit home and we ended our meeting that day on a happy note.

HANDS OF TIME

When I got home, I went immediately to the computer to continue the writing I was working on. Feeling particularly inspired, I got lost in my words. Even so when I looked down at my watch I was astonished to see that 5 hours had gone by since I had sat down to write. As I hurried up and out of my chair to begin regaining my lost afternoon, the clock on the corner of my computer screen caught my eye. It blinked in staunch disagreement with the timepiece on my wrist.

After a bit of crosschecking, it was indeed the watch on my wrist that was in error. In the last hour, it had ticked off five surreal hours of time, while the real world had stayed right on track. And that's how it is in my world…the miraculous collides with the mundane, and there I sit, alone in the mystery, lit from within by my own sacred journey. I felt deeply that day that this was Margaret telling me, "Yes! Yes! Yes!" She was affirming the worth of my notions, and giving me the strength and conviction to continue on with the writing of this book.

HIGHER GROUNDS

After this, Don and I started meeting weekly for coffee and philosophy. Don began chipping away at me with his questions the way a sculptor might chip at a piece of granite, hoping to reveal a grand statue. He did not want foo foo, he wanted proof. Don reasoned that at his worst moments he was just grieving Margaret's death and would come to his senses soon, yet he knew that at his best he was never more than a reluctant believer.

Even so, he was drawn to our conversations like a moth to a flame; he listened patiently to every word, and then fired away with his logical rebuttal. What he seemed to need most of all was encouragement that he was not the only one to go through this odd type of transformation. Although my assurance was appreciated, it became clear that it was the stories that soothed Don the most. Don was reminding me of the healing power of a story. We all have them and we should never underestimate their worth.

One day I was telling Don about the many times I had heard the dying speak of the flying dreams they often had, dreams where they were free of their physical bodies and able to move about unobstructed without pain or burden. The descriptions I have heard from so many at the end of life were so similar, they left me with strong impressions.

It seemed to me that toward the end of life, our energy body is somehow able to tether itself outside of our physical body for brief periods of time. It was as if we received a temporary visa to visit the new land that we would soon be heading to. The inevitable outcome of these flying dreams was that they left my patients with a sense of peace and a belief that they were the sum of more than just their physical bodies.

Don asked me how I knew that these were not simply a type of hallucination caused by the pain medicines often used at the end of life. I told him that of course I could not be sure that it was not this, but that what mattered most is that these experiences gave the dying a sense of peace. He was noticeably frustrated at my lack of evidence, and he grumbled that he was the one who needed a sense of peace right now. With that the story of Tom came to mind, and I began to tell Don his story.

Food for the Soul

Tom was a young man in his middle thirties dying of a rare form of lung cancer. He had never smoked or engaged in any other high risk behaviors, thus his anger at being struck down in his prime was obvious. In seven short months he had gone from being a nationally ranked water skier, to having gained eighty-five pounds in water weight from the steroids used to alleviate his symptoms.

The day I met Tom, we spoke for maybe fifteen minutes before he asked me to leave. Part of my job as a hospice counselor was to start the dreaded conversation about death and dying. Because of the years of research I had done on near death experiences, I often broached this subject with those who were interested in hearing about it.

Each and every time I attempted this with Tom, he would listen intently for a bit, and then abruptly ask me to leave. It actually became somewhat of a game for us. We would chit chat and enjoy each other's company for a bit and then I would inevitably cross the line of his comfort zone, and he would promptly kick me out of his home.

His mother watched our verbal trysts, and would apologize profusely as she showed me to the door each week after I had been booted out by Tom. She would shake her head with a smile, and say that as much as he pretended to be "put over the edge" by our conversations he was inevitably more peaceful after our visits, and she knew he looked forward to them each week.

As the months wore on, I actually was able to get a real dialogue going between us, and I could see the slightest bit of what seemed like recognition in Tom's eyes from time to time. Tom was still kicking me out, but he was also letting me give him a little bit more information, prior to my rapid exit each week.

Tom's physical condition was deteriorating rapidly, and his body had begun to exhibit the telltale signs of system failure. I was not scheduled to see him until later in the week when during a very rushed lunch break, my beeper sounded. It was our clinical coordinator saying that she had just received a frantic call from Tom's mother. Tom was awake and requesting a visit from me, IMMEDIATELY!

When I received this message I was stuck between cars at a notoriously slow, notoriously greasy drive-through restaurant. The minutes seemed like hours as I waited to get through that line. Running on adrenaline, I threw my uneaten lunch on the back seat and headed straight to Tom's house.

When I arrived, the house was very quiet and Tom lay prone in his hospital bed, seemingly unresponsive. His mom was at his side and she looked at me with an expression I could not quite place. She thanked me for coming and then began to tell me how the morning had unfolded.

Tom had become increasingly aroused and had begun to verbalize in a way that she described as similar to sleep talking. At one point he seemed to awaken with a start. He opened his eyes and looked directly at his mother and made a statement that was clear and direct, "Oh my God, this is what she has been trying to tell me. I need to talk to Annette; I need to talk to her now." It was at that point that she had called to have me paged. Shortly thereafter he had quieted down, and had been sleeping ever since.

Hearing these words was like a balm to my soul. I began to talk very softly to Tom, letting him know that I was there and reassuring him that all was as it should be. As I spoke he opened his eyes, and I could have sworn I saw the flicker of a smile cross his face.

He began to speak in a barely audible whisper. I bent to hear his words. It was there I hovered for a moment, poised and ready for what I knew was going to be a profound message. Well profundity is in the eye or in this case, the ear, of the beholder.

He said, "You know what eating that greasy drive-up food will get you in the end, don't you?!"

I stepped back with a start and stared into the mischievous face of my dying friend. He simply winked at me, and then closed his eyes. I quickly looked around the room, searching for the clue of my uneaten lunch bag. My briefcase sat in the corner untouched; I had brought nothing else with me. Tom somehow knew my whereabouts right at the period in time when he was asking to meet with me!

I spent quite a few hours that afternoon with Tom, as he drifted in and out of his body. On several occasions he returned with bits and pieces of information that were later corroborated. Some portion of Tom's consciousness was leaving and then returning to his physical body. At one point his mother had left the house with the unenviable task of picking out a casket in which to bury her only son.

She had been unable to decide between two in particular. Of course Tom should not have been aware of any of this as he lay in his semi-comatose state. Even so, that evening Tom told his mother that he would like the blue box. She had been trying to decide what color lining to have in Tom's casket and she had narrowed it down to two, one of which was blue. Tom died peacefully a few days later.

• • •

RESPONSIBLE PARTY

Don sat still and thought long and hard about what I had just told him. Finally he spoke. "If you had told me this a year ago, I would have thought you were out of your mind, but the things that have happened to me since Margaret's death, especially the white rock…" His voice trailed off and he was lost in a memory known only to him. We sat in heavy silence for a few minutes. I could almost hear the gears in Don's mind grinding away at his old reality, recycling what still had worth and tossing away that which no longer held merit.

I felt empathy for where Don was at. I gently explained to him that with wisdom comes responsibility and he stoically nodded with recognition. I recounted to Don, that as a young woman, when the immensity of the truth hit me, when the continuation of life beyond death moved from a hope to a reality for me, my elation immediately turned to trepidation.

In some ways, this reality is the one thing we all long to know, but the irony of it is that when we actually realize this very personal truth, the outcome is a set of very complex emotions. The first thing I remember feeling was a huge sense of responsibility; the responsibility to live each day with purpose, and to really live my life well. And as this sense of responsibility settled over me, the questions began to fall down upon me like a hard rain—a hard rain that never stops.

The emotions I was describing were just what Don was feeling. He explained that there were moments when he wished himself back to his prior state of blissful oblivion; but these moments were countered by hours of gratitude for the many ways his life had expanded and become more meaningful.

Don's house of truth was under renovation and reconfiguration. Although he was the one who needed to find his truth, he was also eager to know he was not alone in his search. The few stories about others I had shared with Don thus far had calmed him and given him bits and pieces of truth that he was able to assimilate into his expanding world view.

When I asked how I could help Don in his transformation, he said that what he needed most was to hear more stories of others who had walked this path before him. So over the next weeks and months we met at the coffee shop. While patrons ordered cappuccinos and the espresso machines whistled their familiar melody, I spoke and Don listened. Don questioned, and I offered possibilities. Like a weaver at the loom, Don patiently took up the threads of my stories, the sacred stories of those who had gone before us, and he began weaving the fabric that would hold his newborn truths.

• • •

TIME'S UP!

One of the things that Don had always heard about was the way the dying seemed able to choose when to make their final exit. He had heard many anecdotal stories about someone dying who had waited for a final visit from a loved one before letting go. He wondered if I thought it was possible for them to actually choose their time. Thanks to a lovely lady named Nan, I had just the story to answer his question.

Nan was four feet, 11 inches of pure spit fire. At the age of 69 she was approaching her dying in the same way she had approached living: full speed ahead. She didn't let a little thing like a cancer diagnosis rule her world. She enjoyed all of her previously made plans, including a trip to Hawaii that had been planned much in advance. When I questioned her about the wisdom of such a long flight in her poor physical condition, she simply said that she had made a reservation and she intended to keep it. She proved us all wrong. She made that trip to Hawaii, and she came back with a beautiful suntan to prove it!

It was no surprise when, shortly after returning home, Nan let our medical director know that she wanted to be admitted to the hospital. She was again making a reservation, but this time is was for the ultimate vacation destination. Indeed, within hours of her admittance, Nan slipped into a coma, and had begun the dying process, just as she said she would.

During my last visit with Nan, she was unresponsive. As I sat quietly at her bedside, I glanced at the clock on the wall, wanting to be mindful that I was not late for our staff meeting. That's when I noticed that the room clock was not running. I laughed and said out loud, "Your wall clock is stuck at 3:17; are you trying to tell us something?" Of course there was no response, just the labored sound of her breathing.

Later that day I got the call that Nan had died peacefully. The family was on their way up to the hospital but had not yet arrived. Since I was just a block from the hospital and had grown quite close to Nan's daughter-in-law, I decided to be there to greet the family when they arrived.

As I walked into the room, Nan's still body laid before me. A nurse was busy unhooking the oxygen and removing the various intravenous lines, etc. She began to tell me that Nan had spent the first part of the day unchanged, but starting about a half hour ago, her breathing had become very irregular and labored. I stroked Nan's hair and bid her peace on her journey.

The words were not even out of my mouth when a loud commotion filled the room. The nurse jumped and I let out a very audible scream. We turned around to see the clock, which had been repaired earlier in the day, spinning haphazardly on the floor! It had inexplicably fallen off the wall, and was slowly wobbling to a standstill; it was so quiet at that moment you could have heard a pin drop.

But a pin drop is not what I heard. The ticking of the clock is what I heard. I grabbed the chart off the bedside table to see what time had been recorded as the time of death. It was right there in front of me. Nan had died at 3:17, the same moment the clock had been frozen at earlier that morning. I guess this is the time she had made her reservation for!

GRACE AND LATTÉS

One of the things that had left a strong impression on Don was the immense sense of peace that Margaret was able to convey to him shortly before she died. When she had given the white rock back to him that last time in the hospital, she was very clear in letting him know that she had found her own source of peace. She was extremely short of breath and did not give him any details regarding what this feeling of peace was, but he had the feeling it had been profound. He wondered if I had seen others who had been given this same type of grace. The examples of this in my own experience were many, and the stories that day flowed as easily as the lattés.

AN UNSEEN MESSENGER

Melanie was a thirty-six year old woman approaching the end of a three year battle with leukemia. She had been diagnosed with this horrendous disease during her second pregnancy, and her health had rapidly declined in the past few weeks. Very spiritual and open, she talked freely with me about her impending death. She struggled most with the thought of leaving her two young children behind. Ages three and five, she simply could not come to terms with the thought of them growing up without her.

This was an emotionally draining situation for me, because I could so aptly relate to her pain as a mother. For weeks we worked on writing her children letters, which they would receive when they were older, giving them some type of written legacy to connect to her. Although we began this endeavor many times, it was simply too painful for Melanie and she always retreated into her pain, unable to complete this task that was so important to her.

Her physical condition was declining at an alarming rate and I was not surprised the morning her nurse called me saying that it appeared death was imminent. The night before this I had seen two booklets at a local bookstore. They were designed to be given to almost grown children from their mother. I had purchased them with the thought that perhaps they may be useful for Melanie in her quest to leave a written legacy to her children.

When I arrived at Melanie's home, she was lying in bed, too weak to even sit up. Her husband and children were at home, and as I stepped into her room, they all retreated to the kitchen for a break. As our eyes met, she tearfully said, "I waited too long; it is too late to write the kids a message." With that, I pulled out the booklets purchased the night before, and began to read them to her. I openly cried as I read the eloquent messages contained in their pages.

She sobbed and nodded her head, affirming that these words were just what she wanted to say. As I finished the last booklet, she visibly relaxed, and I was glad that perhaps she was finding some peace in the words. With a shaking hand she signed the books to her beloved children. She quieted after a moment and I dried my tears. Then something astonishing happened.

As she lay supine in her bed, perfectly flat, she extended both her arms straight out in front of her and sat bolt upright in bed. I was astonished by the mechanics of this as I observed that her feet and lower body had not moved at all. It was as if something had pulled her up while something else held her feet secure. Whatever this force was, it kept her suspended in this position and she began to gesture wildly. I immediately sensed a new energy envelop the room, and called for her husband to come quickly.

As he and the children entered the room, I moved to the doorway. The scene that unfolded before me to this day remains surreal in my mind. It was as if each member of this family instinctively knew their place. Her husband kneeled down on the left side of the bed. Her three-year-old daughter sat at the head of the bed, and her five-year-old son at her feet. They all looked at her expectantly. She made eye contact with each of them, and then began to look out beyond the end of the bed.

With a strong look of recognition in her eyes, she simply smiled and said, "Oh, I see. Now I understand. I have to go. I have to go now." Clearly not speaking to anyone in this world she repeated this phrase a few more times, then turned to her husband, put her arms around his neck, laid her head on his shoulder and died.

I was absolutely spell-bound by what I had witnessed. Within a matter of minutes, a dying woman had transformed from a mother struggling with the pain of leaving her children to a being who suddenly saw past this grand illusion, finding great peace and acceptance in the process. I had the distinct impression that the transformation had begun when she raised her arms and was lifted by the unseen force.

Because I am a mother, I deeply related to Melanie's torment at leaving young children behind. I had empathically experienced the emotions of each family member as they acted out their parts in the incredible drama unfolding before me. I returned home from work that day inexplicably changed forever, profoundly moved by this experience. The gift Melanie left me with was searing in its contrast to what my reality had been moments earlier. My memory cannot maintain the energy of the experience and although I still quiver at the thought of a mother leaving her children, the chill does not run nearly so deep as it once did.

As so often happens in hospice work, later that week at our staff conference, we processed Melanie's death as a group. It had been an emotionally charged situation for all involved. I shared with the group my experience of having watched Melanie sit straight up in bed, as if something were simultaneously holding her feet, and pulling her torso upward.

After the meeting one of Melanie's nurses, who had also been her long term friend, approached me and asked if we could talk. She had a wide-eyed look of wonder in her face as she began to tell me about an experience Melanie had shared with her.

Very soon after the initial diagnosis of her illness, Melanie had received a nighttime visitor from the spirit realm. She had described this being as "an angel of mercy." This being had placed its hands gently on Melanie's feet, standing at the end of her bed. As Melanie had recounted this experience to her friend, she stated that it had not been her time to go that night, but she definitely knew who it was that stood at the end of her bed holding her feet.

As she finished this story, chills shot through my body. It fit so well with what I had seen that I found it almost eerie at the time. Still, any sense of discomfort this conjured up quickly evaporated as I remembered the look of peaceful recognition that I saw in her eyes that day.

• • •

Soft Focus

As I finished my story, Don's facial expression was soft with memory. I knew he was wondering if, indeed, Margaret had seen her own angel of mercy in the hospital that day. As gentle as the memory of their last conversation was, the recollection of Margaret's last moments of physical struggle weighed on his mind. Although I had not been present for the end of Margaret's life, I had been beside so many others that I knew the scenario well.

The soft focus endings Hollywood shows us are often a far cry from the way real life endings occur. Dying can be hard work, similar to watching a woman give birth but with a different outcome.

Don's next earnest question immediately brought my dear friend Dorothy's memory alive in my mind. As I ushered in her memory, the words began to flow.

BOTTLE IT UP

Dorothy was in her late seventies when the dreaded diagnosis came, ALS or Lou Gehrig's Disease. She had been treated for an array of other things for several months before the actual diagnosis was made. When I met her, she was all of 75 pounds; a toothless imp who scarcely poked her head out from beneath the covers.

Both the admitting nurse and I fell in love with Dorothy the day we signed her into the hospice organization we worked for. Although she was suffering acutely, she still had a twinkle in her eye which hinted at the wisecracking bubbly persona she had once embodied. Her disease process was devastating: completely bed bound and, unable to swallow anything but water, she was essentially starving to death in front of her loved ones.

I arrived at Dorothy's for my weekly visit, surprised at how much weaker she had grown in the past days. Her husband, Jerry, looked drawn and tired so I urged him to go outside and get some fresh air while I relieved his bedside vigil. I heard the front door shut gently as he headed outside for a walk.

My attention immediately fell upon my laboring friend. She looked up at me with eyes as large as saucers, and motioned for a sip of water from a nearby glass. I fumbled at getting the water into her mouth, and I laughed aloud at my inept bedside skills. She smiled weakly and let me know her appreciation through her eyes. She tried to swallow the water, but struggled. Most of the liquid dribbled back out of her mouth, but just enough went down her throat to cause her to choke. Her weak, almost inaudible, cough defied the severity of what was happening. She could not regain her breath and she visibly began to suffer from lack of oxygen. I was panic stricken.

Knowing that Dorothy had requested that 911 never be called for her in an emergency, I rolled her onto her side, and hit her on the back while fumbling for the phone to call in medical help from the hospice team. Dorothy in the meantime ceased struggling and her skin took on a ghostly shade, her lips starting to blue around the edges. After placing my panicked phone call to Dorothy's nurse, I hung up the phone and collapsed in a heap around her. I was certain that she was dying in my presence, and suffering greatly as she did so.

Dorothy regained her breath right about this time. As she took in a shallow yet sustaining breath, her eyes began to dart around the room. The same sparkle I had so loved about her originally was there, and a serene expression radiated from her still pale face. As I began to stammer out an apology for failing to help her when she was choking, her face spread into a slow grin. Although toothless and weak beyond measure, Dorothy turned to me with a voice that was somehow both frail and commanding. The words she spoke burrowed deep within me, "If I could bottle up the joy that I just touched, I would give it to you to take home to your babies, and they would have joy to last them the rest of their days."

Slowly and with great care Dorothy began to recount watching her struggling form from above it, seeing dozens of angels in the room. She was absolutely effervescent with the immense joy the experience had contained. She stated simply that she had come back to her body because her husband wanted to be at her side when she died. Her return was one last act of love she carried out for him.

When Jerry returned from his walk, all looked the same as when he had left. There was no sense in explaining the events that had transpired. When I left Dorothy's home that day, we shared one long soulful glance with one another. Words were inadequate. I could see the peace in her eyes and she could see the gratitude in mine. Dorothy died quietly that night in her sleep held not only in the arms of her husband, but I was certain, in the arms of the angels as well.

• • •

OLD WORLD – NEW EYES

I tried to explain to Don the profundity of the lesson Dorothy had imparted. It was a lesson so powerful that to this day it still makes me emotional to recount it. Dorothy taught me how incredibly inadequate our human eyes are when it comes to seeing the truth. As I struggled to help Dorothy when she was choking, I watched the scene unfold through eyes of fear. Because of this I perceived her to be suffering, when in reality I was the one suffering.

I have no doubt that if I could have looked past the struggle I was seeing in her physical body, I could have looked into her eyes and witnessed her peace. It was I who was incapable of feeling peaceful in the midst of her choking, not her! Dorothy taught me to be a better caregiver to those at the end of life. I learned that if I could detach from my own fear and maintain my peace amidst their struggles that it was synergistic and added to their peace as well.

Don was thoughtful as he took in my words. I could tell that the pieces of the puzzle were starting to come together for him. When I first met Margaret and declined her as a patient and requested her friendship instead, the businessman in him was immediately suspect of my intentions. Margaret had told me how perplexed he was at my benevolence and he kept a watchful eye on my intentions, waiting to discover my real motive.

I could see that Don was beginning to get a glimpse at what fueled my compassionate nature now, and despite his best efforts he was beginning to see real worth in my methodology. From the look on his face, I could see that he could now understand that interactions like the one I shared with Dorothy were worth more to me than any form of revenue in the world.

As the weeks wore on Don's questions became more and more astute. His keen mind began wrapping itself around the semantics of a worldview that contained very real spiritual aspects. The foo foo world, though not a place he wanted to inhabit full time, was now very real to him. The white rock had been a pinnacle experience for Don, yet there continued to be a steady stream of smaller events that kept Don's world view in a state of expansion. At our next meeting, Don asked me if I had ever seen spontaneous healings among the people I had worked with. I had seen one rather miraculous healing, and with Don's prompting, I began to share the story of Vivienne.

20/20 VISION

Vivienne was in her mid-eighties when she signed on with our hospice program to begin her final journey. Her caregiver was her younger sister Violet; of course, younger in this case meant early eighties! The two sisters had been inseparable throughout their lives. Violet, although she was the younger of the two, had always taken care of Vivienne, who had been blind since an early childhood accident. This dynamic had been fertile ground for a very strong spiritual connection between the two.

Vivienne was quite prepared to die, but she did have one unrealized wish. She wanted more than anything to see her beloved sister. She wanted to see her shock of red hair, her bright blue eyes, and the twinkling smile she remembered so well from their childhood. Indeed, the only visual memories that Vivienne had were those of long ago, so she had no idea what her now 83-year-old sister looked like. Violet used to laugh at this and say that Vivienne was better off with her memories, as the real deal was not so "shocking and vibrant" anymore.

As she had been an able caregiver to Vivienne during life, Violet was a compassionate and faithful companion as her sister's days grew short. On a particular morning when Vivienne was relaxed and without pain, Violet gently held her older sister in her arms and sang a song from their childhood. As she sang, Vivienne let her whole being relax into the loving arms of her sister.

Vivienne tentatively reached toward her sister's face, and there, just as she had so many times before, her fingers traced the lines that etched Violet's face. Vivienne closed her eyes, willing her fingers to paint a picture of what her beloved sister looked like. As she opened her eyes, a smile like none Violet had ever seen spread wide across her face. Violet knew in an instant that Vivienne could see.

The two women shared this state of grace for just under two hours. And then, like the setting sun, Vivienne's vision began to dim. Over a period of about thirty minutes her vision once again receded, and she was left without sight. The healing that occurred for Violet and Vivienne that day was without measure. Neither of them could explain the miracle of their experience, yet they found no need to do so. The experience had left them both undeniably altered. Vivienne died very peacefully a short time later, leaving Violet with a gift that no words could aptly explain.

● ● ●

REVOLVING DOORS

Don just shook his head in amazement. He wondered out loud, "Why did these types of things not happen to us in everyday life? And why couldn't Margaret or others like her have been spontaneously healed of their diseases?"

I didn't have the answer to this, but I did have a viewpoint about the true nature of healing. I explained to Don that I had been witness, time and again, to a type of healing that I considered paramount to mere physical healing. Sometimes healing at the body level becomes a moot point when soul healing has taken place. This kind of healing occurs quite often for those at the end of life and it is fairly easy to recognize. I suspected that this is what had occurred for Margaret when she had returned the white rock to Don and told him that her peace was within now.

Don was getting a vague sense of what I was trying to describe but he asked if I had any stories to help him to understand what I meant. With that, soft as a breeze, the memory of Laura sauntered in and took its place at the table beside us. But before I could tell Don about Laura, I first had to tell him about a healing that had happened in my own life many years ago. A healing that made me wonder if the universe had some revolving door system in place.

SEEING THE LIGHT

About six months after beginning my hospice work, I became pregnant with my second child. This was a pregnancy riddled with complications from the outset. With nearly six months remaining until the birth of my child, I was placed on strict bed rest.

My large caseload of clientele was given to other workers and I was sent home. During these months I spent many weeks in the hospital as the physicians worked against my too soon laboring body. During one of the more serious of these hospitalizations, my borders expanded in a most miraculous way.

My labor was progressing despite my physician's best efforts. In response to this I was put on a new medication, which along with slowing uterine contractions can also cause respiratory distress and hypotension. This medication was administered through an IV. My arm began to burn as if fire were racing through my veins.

Before long, I felt as if cement was being pumped into my body. Feeling sluggish and disoriented, I complained to the nurse that I felt as if I could not breathe. She assured me that this was a normal reaction to this medication, and encouraged me to sleep. As I lay there becoming more and more disoriented, a physician who specializes in mind/body medicine, whom I had called earlier in the day, walked into the room.

Although I had never met her, I had left her a message explaining my plight, asking that she see me, should her schedule allow. I tried feebly to express my gratitude for coming to see me. By this time I was slurring my words, and really feeling as if there was a heavy weight on my chest. The nurses had been in and out of my room constantly to check me, but now the door was gently shut and a very calm presence filled the room.

Dr. Peterson simply stroked my face and began to speak very soothingly to me; her intention was to do some clinical hypnotherapy, in the hopes that it would slow the progression of my labor. As her words filled my ears, I felt a tremen- dous sense of peace envelop me. It was as if I was just about to drift into a wonderful deep sleep, when suddenly I found myself hovering above my body.

I was looking down at my swollen body from a vantage point somewhere near the ceiling. I can still see the scene in my mind; my head was turned to the right. Dr. Peterson stood to my left, along with a smattering of monitors and machines. Although I could see that she was speaking to me, I could no longer hear her words. A buzzing sound filled my inner ear and my whole being vibrated to this incredible humming that seemed to come from within.

I felt an extraordinary sensation of movement, swift and smooth…and then all at once, the humming stopped. This was a sensation not unlike what one experiences when diving off a noisy pool deck and into a swimming pool: instant cessation of one sound and instant immersion into another.

I suddenly found myself in the presence of a radiant intelligent light. The experience continued to unfold in ways that are hard to capture with words. I have no idea how long the experience lasted, and I have no clear memory of how I returned to my body. I do know that I spent the remainder of my pregnancy experiencing a state that is best described as "the peace that passeth understanding," and I was absolutely transformed by the presence of this light. The event was deeply personal, and one that I shared only with a few of my very closest confidantes. My newborn daughter arrived early but healthy, and it was not until one of my patients "called me out" that the entire experience began to take on new meaning.

WHERE HAVE YOU BEEN?

Many months after my experience when I did return to work, I had only one client who was still living. In the life of your average hospice patient, my seven month-long absence was four weeks past a lifetime. Feeling deeply reverent at the prospect of being able to finish out the sacred work we had begun together, I entered Laura's bedroom a bit hesitantly. Our medical director had informed me that she had just days left to live, and I knew that physically she would look ravaged in comparison to the last time I had seen her.

As my eyes began to adjust to the dim light, I trained my vision across the room to the bed she was lying in. I was completely unprepared for what I saw. My lovely silver-haired friend laid in her bed radiating the most beautiful iridescent light I had ever seen. I had never experienced anything like this, and I rubbed my eyes thinking I certainly must be imagining this vision. As she turned her head and made eye contact with me, I stood at her bedside stunned. I leaned down and kissed her gently on the cheek, and as I did her hand met mine.

What happened next is one of those things that one can never aptly explain with only words. We simply held each other with our eyes. I felt like I was falling a million miles into her beautiful blue eyes and I could feel her doing the same into mine. After what seemed like an eternity, she smiled and said, "Where have you been?"

I began to stammer out an answer, reciting my pregnancy woes and maternity leave. As I spoke she placed a finger to her lips, gesturing for me to quiet my words. She focused her eyes intently on mine, and once again very evenly spoke the words, "Where have you been?" I did not know what to say, nor did I understand what she was asking. She then answered her own question. With the hint of a smile on her lips, and gesturing broadly around her she said, "The light, this light. You have seen…this same light!!?"

I was stunned. As the tears began to flow, so did the words. I told her how I had somehow left my body and journeyed into a beautiful white light, and how although I had not been near death, it seemed to me like I had stepped through the same doorway as others had at the end of life. She listened, and when I was done, she smiled a knowing smile.

She explained that she too had been at this doorway for several weeks now, and she was certain that the doorway of life and the doorway of death were really one and the same. With her words I began to realize that my trip into the white light had not been ushered in by death, instead it had been ushered in by life…new life, my daughter's new life. In that moment I knew that we need not wait until death to journey into the light; instead, we can choose to live within it. A few days later, Laura left this world full of peace and a wonderful expectancy. My gift to her was offering her companionship on that last journey. Her gift to me was without measure.

• • •

DOORWAYS OF LIGHT

With this story, I began to help Don to see that it was not just death that opened doorways for us. Although the doorway was already cracked open for me, my pregnancy-related crisis was the catalyst that seemed to speed up my personal evolution. I explained that although I believe that living in an expanded awareness is our birthright, most of us do not get there until we are ushered forward by hard-ship.

Don had to agree; it was clearly the loss of Margaret that had ushered in his experience of the white rock. He wondered if I had seen others who had been catapulted forward by their grief. I had without doubt seen how the period of grief and bereavement was often a time of breakthrough spiritual experiences for many. A few stories came to mind. The first was a healing experience that had happened of its own accord during a psychotherapy session.

WARM AND FUZZY

Tina was a fairly regular client of mine. Bright, inquisitive, and nobody's fool, she had been through some difficult times and was currently seeing me as she worked toward healing from the grief of having lost her husband a few months earlier. He had died unexpectedly and Tina was having a hard time putting the pieces of her life back together.

During this particular session Tina was feeling really distraught, like there was no safe familiar place in the world for her. We decided to do some hypnotherapy. My plan was to take Tina backwards in her memory to a time when she felt safe and cared for, to pull those old feelings into her present life. The hypnotherapy was moving along well and Tina was at the point in her session where I had asked her to find a childhood item that brought her great comfort.

She was having a hard time formulating a memory when suddenly I was overwhelmed with the sense that someone else had joined us. Rather than let Tina struggle with her memory, I went with what I was sensing and began to talk Tina through what I was seeing. I described a short and stout gray haired woman who was standing beside Tina, offering her comfort.

Tina was not sure from my description who this could be. At this the woman held up a blue and white checkerboard print blanket which I described. Tina began to cry softly and said the blanket was one she had spent many a night wrapped in as a child. It had been hand knit by her grandmother and when Tina was feeling scared at night her grandmother would wrap her in it and sing her songs until she fell asleep. Tina now knew who the stout gray haired woman was.

After the session Tina and I talked about this uncanny experience. We were both wrestling with our own questions. I had never had a spontaneous visionary encounter like this and I had no idea what had opened the door to it on this particular day. Tina did not understand why it was her grandmother as opposed to her recently deceased husband that showed up to comfort her. The blue and white blanket was clearly the piece of the puzzle that made the experience compelling to Tina, and when she returned home from the session she set out to find that very blanket.

After combing through several storage closets with no success, she finally found it folded deep in the bottom of the hope chest she had received on the day she had married Tom. When she opened up the chest to look for it, what she found were years of keepsakes she and Tom had placed into the chest together.

Weeks later when Tina returned for a follow up session, she described to me how healing it had been to one-by-one go through each memento as she moved closer and closer to the blue and white blanket that rested at the bottom of the chest. She could now see how her grandmother had ushered in the healing of her grief by forcing her to dig deeply into the incredible love she had shared with Tom. Although the blue checkerboard blanket now had a permanent home on the foot of her bed, she needn't use it to quell the winter's chill…for the warmth that Tina was feeling clearly came from within.

• • •

Don thought about the story for a few minutes. He noted that the blanket was a nice touch, but he thought that if Tina's grandmother had really wanted to make her feel warm and fuzzy she would have held up the blue blanket *and* given her the five winning lotto numbers for that week.

I ignored him and then shared another story that hinted at the way grief can be a great healer of great wounds.

A Song for the Ages

Elizabeth had struggled through many years of a stormy marriage. She had married young, a sixties flower child seeking peace and love. Instead what she had found was a marriage full of raging moods and abusive behavior. Her husband had been prone to frequent manic depressive episodes and her life with him seemed to be forever teetering on the edge of chaos.

They had two boys who were now grown into teenagers, and despite Elizabeth's blooming spirituality, her life continued to run in chaotic circles. All of this finally culminated in a violent and tragic death for her husband. She was devastated not so much by his absence, but from the things left undone and unsaid between them.

Many years before his death, Jim had predicted he would die before Elizabeth, and that he had three requests. The first was that he not be put in a suit, the second that no one preach on his behalf, and the third that a certain song be played at his funeral. Tired of his histrionic antics, she half-heartedly listened as he named the song and artist he was requesting. Choosing not to emotionally engage in his drama, she let the words slip right past her, feigning acknowledgment, but remaining in a self-protective fog.

As she sat planning his funeral she was desperately seeking to remember what song it was that Jim had requested be played. Despite hours of combing through their many record albums, Elizabeth could not find the elusive song. She spent hours in prayer, pleading for help to honor this one last request. This seemingly minute event increased her grief exponentially. Her friends and relatives all joined in to help find the song, playing a bit of every song that they owned. Not one of the hundreds of songs sparked any memory for Elizabeth.

As the day of the funeral drew near, she simply surrendered. She was convinced that the loss of this song was just one more aspect of this undone love affair. She went to bed the night before his funeral full of grief and defeat.

It was a bit after four in the morning when Elizabeth woke from a fitful sleep. She was sobbing, lost to the deepest grief she had ever known. She began to pray, asking out loud for help to find the elusive lyric that still escaped her. Without any conscious thought she arose and walked over to the stack of record albums that lay in disarray in the family room. Mechanically, as if invisible hands were guiding her own, she reached into the pile and pulled out an album. Without thought or hesitation, she placed the record on the turntable, picked up the stylus and deliberately placed it on the record. Within seconds the house was filled with the following lyrics:

"In this fading twilight, after all have left your side
One sweet shadow standing by,
One last sweet "I Love You," to echo through the ages
To stir the dusty caverns of the cold heart of time."

Quicksilver Messenger Service
"Call on Me"

To her astonishment, she had placed the stylus precisely on the lyrics which her husband had requested. As she listened to the song in its entirety she realized that this last message was one full of love meant for her alone. With this realization came an almost instantaneous feeling of peace. Had her hand not been guided to this precise point in the song, she would never have found what she was looking for.

Elizabeth explained to me that her grief changed in that one moment in a way that is hard to explain. All of the anguish she had felt regarding unfinished business melted away, and she knew without doubt that she was guided gently in ways she did not understand.

• • •

HEAL IS A FOUR LETTER WORD

At our next meeting I could see that Don was beginning to see that even grief can be healing. Although he was starting to understand where my broad definition of healing was coming from, his quizzical mind was still struggling with the logic of it all.

He was perplexed at why it took the hard edges of life to get us human beings to open up. "Why did soul healing so often wait for the last few days or hours of life to descend upon us?" he wondered. "Wouldn't it be easier to live with a disease process if these healing spiritual events happened earlier in one's struggle?"

I countered that I thought some of these healing events did happen to many at a much earlier stage, but that if a spiritual event unfolds in our lives and we do not have the eyes to recognize it, we will likely remain unchanged. With this came the memory of Lance, a man who harnessed his spiritual vision a bit earlier than most.

MOVING PICTURES

Lance was a fifty-four year old, once burly outdoorsman, who was in the last stages of ALS or Lou Gehrig's disease. On the day I arrived to admit him to the hospice, we made a deep connection. Although he had to be strapped to his wheelchair to avoid slumping over and compromising his airway, he carried himself with an air of dignity. We shared an instant rapport and we quickly formed a friendship that mimicked one forged through years of deep connection. His time left was short and we both talked openly about this.

His primary goal was to begin to embrace his spirituality before his death. He had been raised Catholic, but always had a deep spiritual connection to the earth, which his religion did not seem to fortify.

One day as we sat exploring the nature of reality with our words, he casually mentioned that he had always been able to hear animals approaching him in the wilderness from many yards away. Even something as small as a squirrel made his body vibrate as it approached. He laughed that his friends were always amazed at his accuracy at predicting a vehicle was heading toward their campsite, some unseen miles away. Sure enough, a half hour or so after these predictions, the foretold vehicle would amble by them. He said he could just feel it in his bones.

He also casually mentioned that other parts of nature seemed to talk to him as well. He asked sheepishly if I wanted to see what he meant. Being an eager student, of course I readily agreed to a demonstration. He asked that I wheel his chair into the kitchen. His pantry door was made of a dark, gnarled wood grain. He positioned himself in front of this door, and asked me to stare with him at a certain swirl in the wood pattern.

He began to narrate what he was seeing. "There is a wolf standing near a creek bed, looking toward the West. He is crossing the creek bed and joining three others now. The four of them head up toward a small ridge. As they reach the ridge, they turn, and they stare at us, approving of our watchful eyes."

To my utter astonishment, my eyes were seeing exactly what he described! It was like a monochrome movie within the woods. I stood in stunned silence. We were both taken aback as we realized that I had just shared his vision. We giggled nervously, and I joked to him that now his therapist was as nutty as he was—but our laughter masked a remarkable truth that we had stumbled upon. We had somehow just transcended a border together, even though it had lasted only a moment.

This was a deeply validating experience for him. It was indescribable for me. Lance lived very peacefully for the next four months, and although I never again experienced any visionary phenomenon with Lance, he continued to seek and receive healing from these visionary encounters. He often said that the visions he could see within that gnarled wood door were a big part of his inner sanctum.

A fascinating aspect of Lance's journey was the fact that a few months before he was diagnosed with ALS, he had experienced a lucid encounter with a being from some other realm. It was the source of both comfort and frustration for him. He was awakened from a sound sleep by what he described as an "old Indian." He was dressed in tatters, animal skins and the like. He stood at the end of Lance's bed, and spoke to him in a tongue Lance did not understand.

Feeling no fear, but wanting to see him more clearly, Lance switched on his bedside lamp. The being disappeared as the light came on, and Lance had never seen him again. This troubled him greatly. He had not felt any fear in the presence of this being, and felt there had been great benefit to the encounter, although he could not logically describe what it was. He was hoping to reconnect with this being before his death. This became our goal together.

The last weeks of Lance's life were filled with a myriad of people coming in and out of his home, hypnotherapists, hands on healers, even a Native American Elder. He had encounters with each of them, bringing him to an even more peaceful and faithful state. But his Indian guide did not reappear.

Finally one afternoon, Lance was home alone with his eight-year-old grandson whom he adored. He had wheeled himself into the bathroom, wanting to rinse his mouth of some food he was unable to swallow. In an instant, the mixture of food and water traveled the wrong way in his mouth and he began to choke.

At precisely this same time, Lance heard his two large dogs begin to bark erratically. Seconds later, his Indian friend appeared in the reflection in the bathroom mirror. Lance knew he had come to take him home. Lance welcomed this reunion, until he remembered that he was home alone with his grandson. Telepathically he asked, "Does it have to be this way for Jeremy? I don't want him to find my body." The old Indian nodded his approval, and his reflection faded away. Lance suddenly found that he was once again able to breathe.

He wheeled himself out of the bathroom, and

quickly put a call in to the Hospice medical director. Dr. White and I arrived at Lance's house about the same time. He calmly stated that he wanted to be placed in the hospital that night, that it was time for him to die. Emphatically, Dr. White stated that there was nothing going on physiologically that had not been going on for weeks. She jokingly said, "I'm sorry Lance but I just don't think you're going anywhere tonight."

Lance got his way and was placed in the hospital around five that evening. As we said our good-byes at his house I told him I would try and come by the hospital later, but I had a sick baby at home so my plans were tentative. He smiled weakly at me and said, "I won't be there for long! And when I am gone, I know that somehow I will still be around." With a long hug and misty eyes we parted ways. I never did see Lance as I knew him again. He predicted to his grandson, "that when Family Ties (the TV sit-com) gets over tonight, your grandpa is going home."

Shortly after 9:00 p.m., just minutes after a nurse had checked on a stable Lance, he quietly slipped away. His closest friend Ron, who was a police detective, later told me that when he arrived at the hospital after he had died, the first thing he did was to check Lance's hands to see if they were balled up in fists, indicating struggle. He found Lance lying in bed with his wide open hands resting gently at his sides.

Lance had relaxed into death, just as he had assured me he would. I could almost feel Lance smiling triumphantly as he managed to pull off the dignified death he believed was his birthright.

• • •

REAR VIEW MIRROR

The next time we met, Don was still thinking about Lance. He understood that Lance had begun to live within a larger reality in the months before he had died, but Don wondered if we could choose to live this way sooner. Or as Don put it, before the "grim reaper is gaining ground in the rear view mirror."

I shared Don's quandary and we spent quite a lot of time talking about why we as human beings seem to wait until the end of our days to begin a dialogue with the miraculous. I knew the dialogue was available in our living, because I had found a way to begin it. I knew the beautiful, eloquent communication I shared with the Universe the day I found the stone Madonna was available to each of us. Of this I was certain.

Don smirked and said, "No, you're the Godwoman...the rest of us are mere mortals."

For once I was not willing to engage in our playful banter. "I do not for a moment believe," I said, "that some of us are gifted while others are not. If we want to spread our spiritual wings, we must step off the edge. I am able to "fly" simply because I step off this edge daily. The universe doesn't play favorites; it just plays those who show up for the game."

Don immediately countered that he had never stepped "close to the edge" and the white rock still ended up on his pillow. I disagreed. If losing a life mate, the one you had loved since she was 12 years old, didn't place you on a skinny ledge, I was not sure what did. He quietly shrugged in agreement. I then gently explained that there are others, lots of them, who learn to live on that skinny ledge and spread their wings in their living. With this, the memory of Brad began to soar above us. As Don settled in for story time, I began my tale.

SPIRITUAL BLACK BELT

Brad was the first patient I had who really annihilated my original house of truth. Brad was young and handsome. He was witty and engaging. Brad was also dying. When I met him he was in the last stages of a rare and painful cancer. Young and strong despite his disease, his main symptom was air hunger. Physically he was suffering one of the more difficult deaths that I had seen.

Despite his obvious physical distress there was a palpable serenity about Brad. A serenity I was drawn to in the way a wanderer is drawn to shelter. I sat many hours in his presence, witnessing the unbelievable, watching him transcend the suffering process by accessing a part of himself that was bigger than the suffering. I was transfixed by this. I knew I was sitting in the presence of someone tapping into something greater than himself.

Shortly before Brad died, I gathered my nerve up and I asked him if he would share with me whatever it was that allowed him to walk with such grace upon this very difficult path. It was then that Brad shared his story.

Brad had spent most of his life studying the martial arts. By the time he was in his early thirties he had received the ranking of 10th degree black belt. His entire adult life had been spent cultivating this art. About five years prior to his diagnosis with lung cancer, Brad had begun having very vivid dreams at night. In these dreams he would meet and converse with his sensei or karate teacher. The dreams were so unusual and so vivid that their recall was easy. Brad thought that these dreams were occurring because of his intense focus on his art. And then something happened which Brad said forever altered the way he viewed the world.

During class one afternoon, his karate teacher pulled Brad aside and admonished him for not correctly carrying out an exercise the class had just been taught. When Brad protested that he had only just begun to learn the exercise, his teacher's reply indicated otherwise. He said that he had taught him this same exercise the previous night—during the dreamtime! Brad was astonished. His karate teacher accurately referenced the happenings and the conversation that had occurred in the previous night's dream.

It was on that day Brad learned that he was not his body. After this he and his sensei shared a sacred relationship. They were student and teacher not only during class time, but during dream time as well. During his dying process, Brad was able to access this out-of-body state at will. And although his physical dying process was rigorous, spiritually he was peaceful and serene.

• • •

HOUSE OF STRAW

Although I was a young woman at the time, I was old enough to know my world view was not going to hold up given my life experiences. Brad had helped me to see that my house of truth was made of straw and was not going to withstand the winds of change headed my way. Although nothing in Brad's story fit the way I thought the world worked, I knew with every cell in my being that he was telling the truth. I could feel it. When one sits in the presence of truth, it is tangible. To this day, each time I sit in this presence, it is a brand new, wondrous, indescribable feeling. Like trying to capture a stream of smoke in your hand…it is fleeting and elusive, but you know it exists.

Brad was the first of many to knock down my boundaries. The first time the walls came down it took my breath away. Soon, it became a regular event, one I actually began to enjoy! I met truly great teachers in the dying every day, but Brad stood out. He was part of a fairly elite group among these teachers. Brad had not waited for death to introduce him to the greatness of his being, he had discovered it through his living, and this in itself had completely transformed his dying process. In many ways I was still a kid, just twenty-four-years old, but I had the eyes to see this. I knew that I, too, wanted to live my greatness rather than wait for death to expose it.

It was at this early stage of my life that I began to cultivate a conscious relationship to the universe. I began learning the power of introspection, harnessing the right use of intention, and building a personal repertoire of metaphor around which to shape my world.

The next time we met for coffee Don could hardly contain himself. Before I could say a word, with raised eyebrows and a sarcastic lilt to his voice, he asked, "Do I look a little tired to you, Godwoman?" I cautiously responded that indeed he did look a little spent. He was incredulous as he began his haughty response, "Well, you would look tired too if you had all this foo foo s - - t happening to you at night!" That day I was the one who got to sit back and listen to a story unfold. He looked both ways as if he was about to cross a dangerous street, and then he began to talk.

FRIENDLY FIRE

Grief had not shown itself to be much of an insulator against stress for Don, and since Margaret had died he often felt himself uptight and anxious at the end of the day. When Don was stressed, he enjoyed relaxing in the tub. Indeed, one of his favorite spots in his home was the Jacuzzi in the large garden bathroom that he and Margaret had shared.

As he readied the bath, he smiled at the memory of the playful contention that always surrounded this ritual when Margaret was living. For years, Don's chosen form of relaxation had been to climb into the jetted tub with a book, while Margaret preferred to relax by watching TV in bed. The bathroom adjoined the bedroom without a dividing door, so when both Don and Margaret were relaxing at the same time, the verbal rounds of friendly fire would begin!

As the Jacuzzi jets roared to life, up went the volume on the television. Inevitably while Don was hollering for her to turn down the volume so he could relax, Margaret was hollering for him to turn off the bubbles so she could hear the TV. Like painted ponies on a carrousel, round and round they would go, each filled with the amicable exasperation that comes only from years of truly and deeply loving your partner, flaws and all. That night without Margaret there to play her part, the house seemed terribly quiet.

As Don settled into the tub he sat for just a moment in the silence. He toyed with the idea of leaving the bubbles off as a gesture to Margaret, but before sentimentality could ensnare him, his logic was sprung free by his exhaustion and a sore back. As he leaned over to turn on the jets he was feeling smug at having redeemed himself from such a foo foo thought. Then he heard a loud burst of noise from the bedroom.

Startled, he jumped up and out of the tub and slid on the tiled floor as he grabbed for his towel. Before he even made it out of the bathroom he could see the familiar blue-white glare of the TV dancing off the bedroom walls. He stood still as a statue. The television blared loudly, playing its raucous symphony to an empty room. With no one at all to share the absurdity of it with, he stood there in the commotion unable to hear anything but the pounding of his own heart.

In this final round of friendly fire, Margaret had certainly launched a successful ambush. As Don walked slowly back to the bathtub, he thought to himself that his white towel may as well be a white flag; for he was truly learning to surrender to a reality that was much bigger than he had ever imagined.

As Don finished his story, I had a hard time suppressing my laughter. "It's not funny," he insisted. As he went to refill his cup of coffee my prolonged laughter trailed behind him like the tail on a kite. With his gilded New York accent, I could hear him muttering something about how "non-freakin' therapeutic" the Godwoman was during his time of greatest need.

When he returned with his full cup of coffee, I held my amusement in check and I asked in earnest what I could do to help. "Just shoot me and put me out of my misery." When I queried whether he was being funny or if misery really described how he felt, he was quick to respond with a very sincere tone. "Annette how can you explain this stuff? Am I losing my mind? Is my house haunted? What the hell do I make of all this foo foo?" I patiently explained that these types of things happened to other people that I had worked with, too. I had seen it so often I even had a name for it: grief related electrical sensitivity syndrome.

"Wonderful," he said glibly, "Now you are branching out into rocket science too?" Not amused, I asked if he cared to read my 200 page doctoral dissertation that researched similar phenomenon associated with near death experiences. He declined and sheepishly asked if I could just give him the cliff notes version now.

I then described that in my twenty-plus years of working with the dying and their families, I have heard these types of electrical oddities recounted by the hundreds. A sudden electrical blip will occur just as the bereaved are having a sense of their loved one being near. Lights will blink, clock radios flash, electronic devices turn on or off of their own accord. Of course, I cannot explain the phenomenon, but I have been able to build a personal philosophy around these events in which to hold my experiences.

I explained this philosophy to Don: quantum theorists teach us that energy can never be destroyed. So when the human body dies, the energy body must live on in some other form. Grief related electrical phenomenon occurs when the energy body of the deceased is nearby. This otherworldly presence somehow interrupts the electrical circuitry of this plane, and although we cannot see their energy, we see the effects of it in the three dimensional electronic world around us.

Don grinned widely, and opened his mouth to speak. Before he could make another rocket scientist joke I held my hand up to abate him. We both laughed and trying to keep a straight face I said, "From now on just call me Dr. Godwoman, ok?"

TRUE NORTH

As the weeks wore on, Don began to seem more and more comfortable in this new world he was exploring. When I asked how he was doing, he grew quiet, as if he were measuring his words. When he finally spoke he said that if he really had to choose one word to describe how he felt, he had to admit—that beneath all of his "anti-foo foo" rhetoric—what he truly felt was peaceful. He was very up-front about admitting that if he did not have me mentoring him through this time, he would likely be feeling something entirely different.

Over the previous months of our friendship Don had gotten to know me pretty well. Sometimes our coffee talks spilled over into the noon hour and it was not unusual to find him and my husband talking stock options at our kitchen table while I fixed lunch and supervised the busy life of two teenagers and a newborn.

Don could see that I managed to live a pretty normal life despite my obvious foo foo "disability." He respected this more than he wanted to admit, and he wondered out loud if maybe I could teach him how to do the same thing. I explained to Don that I would love nothing more than to help him to navigate well in his new world, but I cautioned him that the map was big, and everyone's path was different. He understood what I was telling him and sheepishly asked, "Can you at least help me find my compass?" Unbeknownst to Don, he had just taken his first step on his own by engaging in the language of metaphor.

PART THREE

CALLING OVERSEAS

Our coffee time meetings took on a little different tone after this. I began in earnest to share the things I had learned with Don. It was ironic that it was Don who had been armed with poster board and flow charts those many months ago when Margaret first pinned the two of us together in the same room.

These days, I was the one arriving with volumes of material. My material however, was not as succinct as what Don was used to. It was not neatly printed on poster board, nor was it easily accessed via flip chart. My personal brand of life-wisdom usually showed up by way of sudden inspiration and was therefore often hastily written on whatever scrap of paper was available in the moment. This haphazardly written self chatter was meaningless to everyone but me. Indeed, this collection of errant paper compromised nothing less than my entire life's philosophy.

One by one I shared with Don my stories, my memories, and my musings; in essence, the nuts and bolts that held my house of truth together. Don combed through my myriad of offerings with a mixture of pity and reverence. Sometimes he was genuinely touched by what he was seeing. Other times found him casting a woeful glance my way, as he read aloud with mock aplomb, one of the heartfelt musings that I had built my life around.

One day Don picked up a bright purple business card that read, 'Clairvoyant Medium.' He flashed a smile like the cat that had caught the canary. He read the words aloud and laughed, commenting smugly that even the Godwoman must need a little help placing her "overseas" calls once in a while. He had seen enough primetime television to know that a 'medium' is one who talks to the dead. Why he wondered, would I pay someone money to give me additional information from the other side, when I clearly lived within a continual stream of it as it was? He said that he was certain the shows he had seen on television were staged anyhow. As I grabbed the business card from his hand, the memory of Johnnie R. began falling down like a soft rain.

SINGING IN THE RAIN

Cynthia, a co-worker of mine, had been listening to my accounts of Renee's ability to tune into those on the other side for several months. Renee was a clairvoyant medium, and made her living talking to the dead. Cynthia finally decided to visit this woman herself, and I accompanied her, hoping that I would once again witness something magical.

As Renee began her reading, she immediately tuned into a gentleman in his late 60s who was very eager to talk with Cynthia. Bingo! A long term, absolutely beloved patient of Cynthia's had died weeks before and we were both hoping to receive a message from him.

As Renee continued to tune in, she began telling Cynthia things that did not seem to fit, mentioning dancing in particular. As far as Cynthia knew, Johnnie had no love of dancing; at least he had never mentioned it to her. Cynthia told Renee this did not seem descriptive of Johnnie. Renee held her ground saying he is definitely showing her a dancing scene, something akin to "Singing in the Rain."

As Cynthia's disappointment grew, Renee's level of insistence gained ground as well. Finally Renee asked out loud for more clarification on what Johnnie was trying to tell her. With a very quizzical look on her face she turned to Cynthia and said, "He wants me to tell you that he doesn't have to wear shoes in the shower anymore—THAT is what he had been trying to show me."

I thought for sure that this would be the final straw for Cynthia and that she would walk out of the reading. I looked down at my friend to see her pale and still. She looked no different than an accident victim who had suddenly slipped into the gray abyss of shock. After a moment she composed herself and began to tell the following story.

"As Johnnie's nurse, I had grown extraordinarily close to him in the last weeks of his life. As his health deteriorated I became intimately involved in his care. Because he was no longer able to bathe alone, I had become privy to Johnnie's bathing routine. Although this is all in a day's work to a nurse, there was a secret component of this ritual known only to myself and Johnnie. You see, Johnnie was a war veteran. He had vivid memories of a fungal infection that had swept through his army barracks and terrified him. As a young soldier he had to shower with his army boots on, to avoid catching this horrible infection.

Although long home from the war, it seems Johnnie had never been able to eradicate his paranoia of contracting this fungus. Because of this, he simply could not bear the thought of bathing without shoes on. When his health deteriorated to the point of needing assistance with his bath, he had no choice but to share his secret obsession with me. I had never told a soul about this, out of respect for Johnnie."

• • •

You Have Mail

This opened up a whole discussion between Don and I about mediums and their authenticity. It was a question I had spent considerable time wrestling with myself. I knew that in my life, communication with those who have died had shown itself to be a reality, but when these communications occurred it was not due to a summons on my part.

Early on in my hospice work I did visit the medium mentioned above on a regular basis. It almost became a type of therapy for me. Not all of my visits to her were like the one I detail above. Many of them brought me vague information that I could tinker to suit my needs, in essence leaving me with a weak message from some departed soul I had worked with.

But then there were times like the one above that just absolutely left me with no doubt that there is a way to receive messages from the other side. Visiting Renee was a productive pastime for me at that stage of my life for several reasons. The first was simply the therapeutic value of believing that there was a better place waiting for those I saw suffering. I was a young woman who watched people die day in and day out and I needed to put my faith in something beyond death.

When I would visit Renee and she would have a 'direct hit' like the one she had with Johnnie R., it was like a balm to my soul. It helped me to continue to do my work with the belief that there is healing waiting for all of us, regardless of how illness or infirmity may ravage our bodies.

The second positive impact that visiting Renee had on me was that it left me with a sense of expectancy that there might be one more message waiting for me from those I had worked with and cared for. I think this attitude of expectancy is what initially opened the door for me to have communications with the other side. Visiting Renee allowed me to hold open the possibility that these types of communications were possible. Each time she gave a reading that deeply affirmed this, my horizon of belief expanded, allowing me to see farther and farther into the other side.

Don stopped me mid-conversation and asked if I actually thought spiritual messages were so fragile that it required belief on the part of the ones left behind in order for a message to get through. I told him that I thought messages from the other side were like radio waves, and that they can be sent regardless of belief. But if a message is sent and there is no belief present in the intended recipient, it is like radio waves being bounced off a radio receiver that is turned off—the radio waves simply rebound away, essentially unheard. His question immediately brought the story of Becky to mind.

HEART SHAPED BOX

Becky was an acquaintance of mine who had lost her teenage daughter Jill in a tragic boating accident. Jill had been her only daughter and Becky's grief had completely consumed her. Before long Becky was a mere shell of the vibrant woman she had once been. She could find absolutely no joy in her life since her daughter's death and she had completely lost faith in everything. Her friends had been trying for months to bring Becky out of her dark night with no success.

Mutual friends had suggested that Becky and I go to lunch together in the hopes that one of my other-world stories might stir the energy of healing within her. During this lunch I did my best to open a doorway of hope for Becky. I told her of a few of my first hand experiences that hinted at the continuation of life after death, yet she met my words with no more than a vacant stare. She then told me that she did not believe in any of this.

Becky then began to tell me that the week prior to this, she had had a phone reading with a well known medium. Having waited months for the appointment, she was deeply disappointed in the outcome. This had added to her staunch non-belief in messages from the beyond. The medium shared some vague information with Becky that had felt much too general to derive any real healing from. Becky felt that she had been taken advantage of, and said there had been no worth to the session at all.

Most frustrating of all to Becky was the fact that the medium kept telling Becky that Jill was holding a beautiful silver heart shaped box in her hands, and gesturing that it belonged to her mother. Becky could make no meaningful connection to the heart shaped box. Jill had been a real tomboy and never owned anything even remotely resembling that which the medium was describing. Becky hung up the phone feeling even more lost and disillusioned than before.

As Becky told the last part of this story my breath caught in the back of my throat. I could feel a surge of energy rising up within me as I bid Becky to stay seated while I ran to my car for just a moment. As I walked the short distance to the parking lot, my feet hardly touched the ground.

Just before meeting Becky for lunch that day as I was leaving my office, one of my colleagues approached me in the parking lot. I had not yet said hello when she pushed a small gift bag affixed with a bow into my un-expectant hands. Before I could protest this unwarranted gift she was backing away saying, "In a rush, don't have time to argue! Just call it your lucky day. I was walking by a boutique this morning and this little trinket was in the window calling your name." With that she was gone.

I had opened the bag as I drove to meet Becky. Underneath the bow, nestled on a piece of red tissue paper sat a beautiful heart shaped silver box. It was really lovely, but I was perplexed at why my colleague had given it to me. Now, as I opened my car door, the bag lay just as I had left it on my car seat, but the sil- ver box had taken on new meaning.

The enormity of it all washed over me as I realized the incredible symphony of events that had taken place for this silver box to find its way to Becky. I felt like a sacred messenger, honored and humbled at the same time. I returned to our lunch table absolutely glowing with expectation, certain that Becky's heal- ing would begin in this moment.

Before handing the bag to Becky I recounted to her the morning's events with my colleague. I did not however, reveal to her what the mystery gift was. I motioned for her to open the bag. I sat expectantly waiting to see the recognition in her eyes. She peered into the bag and forced a weak smile. "This is very nice of you. Thank you."

With that she let the red tissue paper fall over the box again, and she gently placed the bag on the table beside her. I was dumbfounded. I asked if she could see the significance of this, to which she replied simply, "Not really. Jill was a tomboy and would never have liked something like that box."

My words were of no use. Nothing could penetrate the darkness that had completely consumed Becky's world. The heart shaped box may as well have stayed untouched in that storekeeper's window, for Becky was truly unable to see its beauty. Her grief was so deep, and her belief so frail, that her heart was as hollow as the beautiful silver box.

● ● ●

I could see the recognition in Don's eyes. He commented that it really didn't matter what kind of radio waves were being sent to us if our tuner was turned off. I agreed wholeheartedly. Lest he lose himself to the foo foo, Don casually leaned back in his chair and began his philosophical questioning, "So do you think this is why wizards wear those tall purple hats, 'cause it helps their radio reception?" I just shook my head and laughed. With Don Borwhat it was clearly one step forward and two steps back.

LOST IN TRANSLATION

Even though our last meeting had ended with Don's bad wizard humor, he had clearly been thinking about what we had spoken of. He was still trying to wrap his head around the concept of the dead being able to send their messages through a medium. Don's only experience of mediumship had been to watch some of the popular television shows which utilize a live audience and a medium that is able to pick up a variety of messages during the show. These shows were particularly frustrating to him, as he felt like the messages were often convoluted. He always felt particularly irritated when the mediums identified people by their middle names as opposed to first names.

He thought this added to the entire suspect nature of the whole concept. Although I could appreciate his frustration, I could also relate to the once-removed type of communications that mediums seem to be most privy to. I explained to Don that in my own experience of otherworld communication, that direct translation is very difficult. I told him that on the occasions when I have received communications from the other side, it is almost like listening to a conversation under water, or even trying to read something that is written underwater.

Indeed, for me spiritual communications are easier to describe with symbolic language as opposed to literal. I reasoned that perhaps there is a basis for mediums so often using information that is just shy of direct, like using a middle name in place of a first name, or referencing a small seemingly insignificant event rather than an obvious one. Maybe this is due to the difficulty of sending minute details from the other side, perhaps it is the details that get lost in translation. He asked if I could give him an example of how this had played out in my own life, and the following story came to mind.

• • •

SMOKE SIGNALS

Having been raised in a large multi-generational family, I had the privilege of enjoying a very close relationship with many of my older relatives. Only one of my grandparents lived long enough to see me bring my own children into the world, and this was my ornery, loveable paternal grandfather Louie. "Gramps," as I called him, was 93-years-old when I gave birth to my first child. My son and I would visit my grandfather often and I dearly loved watching the interplay between them.

My grandfather died when my son was just a toddler, but he had enjoyed enough awareness of his great-grandfather's presence to have a fond and clear memory of him. One day, several months after his death, as my son sat playing, I saw him making the telltale hand gestures of one who was smoking. I was alarmed to say the least at seeing my toddler mimic a chain smoker and I rather sternly asked him who he had seen doing that.

Without hesitation he said, "I saw Great Grandpa today. He was standing by the 'frigidator." My grandfather was a lifelong smoker, and I did have a photo of him smoking his pipe. Was my son just pretending to play with his great grandfather, or had he actually been paid a visit by him? I wasn't sure so I prodded my son a bit.

"Why was Great Grandpa smoking?" I asked. My little boy looked up at me with his perfect round clear eyes and said simply, "So he could blow smoke in my ear."

As my son spoke these unusual words, the memories of a forgotten interaction I had shared with my grandfather began falling in succession, like a carefully lined row of dominoes.

As I had visited with my grandfather on this day,

my son was unusually fussy and tugging at his ear. When my grandfather asked what was wrong, I explained that I was afraid the baby may have an ear infection and that I was planning on taking him to the pediatrician later that day. My grandfather motioned for me to bring the baby to him.

As I neared him, he began to retrieve his beloved tobacco and pipe from the pocket of his pants. I responded abruptly, "What are you doing?"

To which he replied matter of factly, "Gonna blow a little smoke in his ear." Well, I may have been a naïve 24-year-old first time mother, but there was no way anyone was going to blow tobacco smoke in my precious little boy's ear. My grandfather tried to explain his rationale, but being an overprotective young mother, I was having none of it and I promptly ended the entire conversation. (I now know it was his version of a natural healing technique called ear candling).

I saw the pediatrician later that day; the ear infection was treated with antibiotics and I never even thought of this blip of a conversation with my grandfather again. Until now, when my toddler said the phrase, "blowing smoke in my ear." My mind raced as I did the math. My son was only months old when the interaction occurred and he could never have remembered it; of this I was certain. Now this long forgotten conversation, as quirky as it was brief, was one I would cherish for the rest of my days. I turned to resume watching my son navigate busily in his imaginary world and my heart was full of gratitude for having been given the gift of seeing life for a moment through the eyes of my child.

• • •

Don shook his head and laughed, "So your grandfather returns from the grave with a message, and rather than telling you where he hid the family fortune he decides to blow smoke in your little boy's ear?"

"Pretty much!" I replied with a smile.

Native Tongue

In all seriousness I continued to emphasize to Don how very often the spiritual messages I had been privy to came across in these odd, uncanny ways that were always just a bit shy of direct. In my work with grieving families, I had often seen that, like my son, children were able to be messengers of the mysterious. Don asked me why I thought this was.

"Perhaps it's their innocence which allows the

messages to come through so cleanly," I said. "As we grow and our critical minds begin to engage, we begin to heavily filter the subtle perceptions that come our way. Let's just say that a message from the other side is like a soft piece of clay. When the message is sent from the other side, it is loosely formed; soft, warm, and malleable. If the message is received by hands that are rigid and unyielding, the nuances, the details carved into the clay are immediately lost in the tight grip of our logic. The original message is hardly decipherable, if it is recognizable at all. A child, so full of innocence, receives the soft clay with warm gentle hands…hands that leave the original shape unmarred so that it can be brought intact into their still magic-filled world."

The metaphor made sense to Don, and instead of his usual smart aleck comment, he actually waxed poetic for a moment as his mind opened around this concept. He reasoned that perhaps as we approach the end of our lives, we once again become childlike in our ways, and in doing so are able to open up to the subtle realms.

I nodded my head approvingly, and my eyes grew soft at the notion of how very far Don had traveled in these last months. He saw my wash of emotion and immediately chastised me for not only being foo foo, but for being pathetic as well.

FLUENT IN METAPHOR

As we sat down for coffee the next week, Don said he had been thinking a lot about the symbolic messages that seem to be part of this otherworld communication. Although he appreciated the language of metaphor, he wondered if I ever got messages that were in plain English.

There had been a few times where I had been guided as sternly as if a hand were actually on my shoulder. Each time this had occurred it had been in the presence of danger. I had sometimes bemused myself by reasoning that my guardian angels did not always have time for me to follow the breadcrumb trail and this is when they brought out the cosmic two-by-four. When Don pushed me for details I recounted the following story from my youth.

• • •

CRASH COURSE

It was a typical youthful outing. My friends and I were enjoying our usual teenage shenanigans when suddenly a voice told me in very clear terms that I needed to go home. Not later, but now. It was as if someone had just taken me by the shoulders and forcefully directed me to go in the other direction. I had heard this inner voice before and I was beginning to clearly recognize that it only spoke to me when the information was really vital. Even though I was just a teenager this inner voice gave rise to a lingering bent toward introspection that continues in my life to this day.

On this particular night I was climbing into a car with seven of my friends, when suddenly this voice told me to get out of the vehicle and walk if I had to. To the dismay of my friends, I refused to get in the car with them. They left me standing there alone, as they drove away to continue their evening. Minutes later when I heard the low moan of a siren in the distance, I knew what had happened.

I summoned a ride straight to the hospital, knowing that is where my companions were headed. Indeed, just moments after I had been told to vacate that vehicle, it was involved in a serious accident, slamming into a large boulder. Fortunately no one lost their lives, yet each person in the vehicle received serious injuries. Although grateful for the insight this inner knowing allowed me, I was on this occasion also plagued with confusion and guilt. While my best friend endured surgeries and many months on crutches, I had remained unscathed. My protection had been a source I did not yet understand.

• • •

Don said he thought this same voice had warned him on the day Margaret first introduced him to me. Unfortunately he had not listened, and now look where it had gotten him! I shrugged away his bad humor and continued on with another example of no-nonsense communication from the other side. This occurrence had reminded me that sometimes a spade is just a spade.

KERNEL OF TRUTH

It was a crisp October morning and my husband's beloved grandfather, Grandpop, lay dying in a local hospital. Brian had been Grandpop's go-to guy while he struggled through the last hard years of living with congestive heart failure, and Brian was not about to leave Grandpop's side now.

On this morning, Grandpop lay in the same semi-comatose state he had been in for the preceding twenty-four hours. Closing the door behind him, Brian moved close to his grandfather and began to say all of the things he most wanted him to hear before leaving this world. There was a long litany of thank yous and I love yous before my gentle-giant of a husband finally broke down in a heap of sobs next to Grandpop's laboring body.

Quite unexpectedly, Grandpop began to rouse, and a startled Brian quickly tried to regroup and wipe the tears from his face. Grandpop opened his eyes just long enough to look Brian in the eye for one brief second. He excitedly announced that he was, "gonna get out of here!"

Brian gently asked, "Where do you need to go, Grandpop?" Brian's question hung in the air for only a moment before Grandpop's matter of fact reply: "I'm gonna go get some popcorn." Brian was afraid he might actually try to get out of bed, so he attempted to soothe his grandfather by saying, "You can get some popcorn later; for now I just want you to rest." If there was anyone that Grandpop always listened to, it was Brian, and true to form, he settled right back down and fell into a slumber that he would never really rouse from again.

As Grandpop lay sleeping, Brian phoned to give me an update on how things were going at the hospital. He lamented that Grandpop was in and out of consciousness and not making a whole lot of sense. Brian and I had talked a lot about the symbolic language the dying use, and Brian expressed his disappointment that the things his grandfather muttered did not seem prophetic at all. He said there had been only one really clear statement and of all things, it was about leaving the hospital to get some popcorn. My sadness for Grandpop's struggles disappeared in that moment, as a memory clear as a new dawn warmed me with its light.

Six weeks earlier, I had been awakened in the night with a very odd visit. The visitor was Brian's grandmother. I had never met her, but I had heard a lot about her. She was a beloved and much missed part of the family. She had died ten years previously and not a day went by that Grandpop did not remind us all that he wanted to find his way back to her. At the time of the dream I was totally perplexed. Grandmom had appeared and very insistently offered me a bowl of popcorn. I had heard many heart-warming stories about her, but none of these stories had a thing to do with popcorn. I was puzzled, as I could feel there was a message being given, but I did not have the means to decode it. Unable to extract any meaning from this dream, I drifted back into a fitful sleep.

Three more times in the next hour, this same sequence of events repeated. It was as simple as it was perplexing. Grandmom stood before me in a green dress with a bowl of popcorn in her hands. That was it. There was nothing else to the dream. By the third repetition of this I was absolutely certain that this was a message, and not just a dream. Flustered by my inability to make sense of the input I was getting, I gently nudged my husband awake. He listened groggily and shook his head "no" when I asked him if there was any significance at all to popcorn and his grandmother. I asked if his Grandpop loved popcorn. Again he answered in the negative. He added, "They loved ice cream. If Grandmom had been holding a bowl of ice cream, that would make sense, but popcorn? It just doesn't fit."

Although I pushed him a bit to search for something that might explain the odd picture I was seeing, try as we may, in the wee hours of the morning, the meaning of this dream remained elusive. As Brian fell back to sleep, I was quite bothered by my inability to derive meaning from this occurrence. My skill at reading the symbolic language that is such a part of the other side is normally quite honed, but this time I was at a loss. Since I could derive no logical meaning from the dream, my mind flipped into metaphor mode and that is when I turned on the light to write my thoughts in my dream journal.

Before Brian could express much more disappointment at his grandfather's choice of final conversation topics, I had already made my way into our bedroom to retrieve my dream journal. I very animatedly reminded him of our dialogue that night just a few weeks before when I had awakened him with my odd questions about popcorn. With just a moments prompting, the memory returned to him in full force. The enormity of it hit us both and the phone line grew quiet as we sat in the sacred silence that comes from truth. With a shaking hand I flipped the journal to a page dated six weeks before. I read the entry aloud to him over the phone:

(actual entry)
September 2
1 a.m.

Can't sleep; mind won't turn off... Recurring dream / visit... Grandmom is showing me a bowl of popcorn, holding it out, insistent. Is this message or metaphor? I wake Brian and ask what is the significance of popcorn with Grandmom... He says there is none. I push him for other explanations...he has none... He is now back to sleep... I am still perplexed. Is this metaphor???

Kernel of corn, hard, indigestible. When exposed to hot oil, it transforms into something that can nourish. Message... Our bodies are like these kernels of corn, hard shells that hold something precious (our souls). When the kernel (our body) is exposed to hot oil (pain / suffering / death) our soul is released (popcorn).

Still perplexed... will let it go now—time will show what is true.

As is so often the case with nighttime reveries, the

next morning I failed to recall the night's adventure. Apparently so did my husband, as the popcorn conversation never surfaced between us again until the morning Grandpop lay dying.

Grandpop's last conversation with Brian not only made sense of this odd dream, it also eased our sadness and reminded us that Grandmom was right there to greet him. And although the metaphor I had stretched around the dream in my journaling was thought provoking, I had to laugh at my blunder. This time the kernel of truth I was searching for laid no deeper than the bottom of the popcorn bowl.

• • •

Don snickered. "So even the Godwoman overshoots her target once in while, huh?" I laughed along with him and agreed that, indeed, I had stretched for meaning on this one, when all I really had to do was wait.

"So let me ask you this Godwoman. If Grandmom is going to offer you a bowl of something from the other side, why not offer her and Grandpop's favorite: ice cream?"

"Don, I think she was brilliant in her delivery. If Grandpop had talked about ice cream while he was dying, we wouldn't have thought twice about it. We would have thought he was simply reminiscing about a part of life that he had really enjoyed. There would be no otherworld tingle to it. I think Grandmom knew this, so she picked something so offbeat that it really made me stop and pay attention. When Grandpop said the word popcorn as he lay dying, it was like Grandpop and Grandmom wrapping Brian and I in a blanket of peace. Although popcorn would have meant nothing to someone else, it was the most beautiful parting word he could ever have spoken to us."

Don conceded that what I was saying seemed plausible, but he still had questions. "So how do you know the difference between a simple dream and a message? I have dreams of Margaret all the time. Some of them make no sense at all, and other times they bring me a lot of comfort."

It was a complex question, and one I did not have an easy answer to. I explained to Don my belief that our sixth sense is like a muscle and the more we use it the stronger it becomes. "Keeping a dream journal right next to your bed, and taking the time to write down each night's dreams is the best way to decipher the long-term meaning of a dream. The simple act of paying attention does a lot to filter the important messages from the simple misfiring of a mind in the dream state."

Don quickly dismissed my suggestion and said that the only thing he planned on keeping on his nightstand was the remote control and a glass of water in case he got thirsty.

I deflected his stubborn retort and simply said, "So to answer your question, I have had direct messages, but they have been few and far between."

Despite a few instances of direct messages, for the most part metaphor and symbolism were the codes I had learned to crack when it came to dialogues with the universe. I explained to Don that in my life, there were certain symbols that had become highly charged with meaning. These symbols were comprised of many things: places, people, sayings, animals, etc., all sharing the common ground of having been part of a great life lesson that had deeply affected my life. I used these symbols as teachers and messengers, and they often spoke to me in truly uncanny ways. When he asked for an example, frog jumped right into my thoughts.

GET IN MY BELLY!

On my 39th birthday I was feeling a bit melancholy. For the past ten years I had desperately wanted a third child, but the complicated Rubik's Cube that had been my life never allowed me to get all the squares lined up. I had vowed that once I hit my 40th year, I needed to move past this desire and let it go. So as my 39th birthday dawned, I was looking at the calendar and wincing.

I was in love with a man who also wanted a child, and our relationship had been the most balanced and happy one I had ever known. Even so, anytime the conversation of marriage came up between Brian and me, I broke out in a cold sweat before he even had to! Despite our mutual desire for a child, we both ignored the pink and blue elephant in the living room.

Needless to say when I woke up on the morning of my thirty-ninth year, my biological clock was ticking rather loudly. I was sincerely saddened by both the unrealized desire for a child, and my unwillingness to move past my fear of marriage.

I was not in the mood to celebrate, so despite several invitations by well meaning friends and family members, I decided to spend the day alone. I drove to a picturesque little town about an hour from where I lived, and spent the day wandering through its quaint boutiques and galleries. My intention was to buy myself a birthday gift to buoy my flagging spirits, but I had no idea what that gift might be. I wandered from boutique to boutique, never really knowing what it was that I was seeking.

And then my eyes fell upon it! A tiny pewter frog

sat in perfect splendor before me. As I picked up the figurine and inspected the two tiny frogs which sat upon the larger frog's back, a fable that had been one of the greatest teachers in my life began to filter through my thoughts.

The fable tells of a frog and scorpion who are sitting at the river's edge. Scorpion wants more than anything to get to the other side of the river, but he cannot swim. He asks frog if she would be so kind as to let him ride upon her back across the river.

Frog answers, "How do I know you will not sting me?" Scorpion says, because then we would both die. With this, Frog gives her trust to scorpion, and lets scorpion climb upon her back.

Half way to the other side, scorpion plunges his barbed tail deep into the soft flesh of frog's back. Before she dies, frog asks, "Why scorpion? Why did you sting me?"

Scorpion just twitches his tail and says, "I stung you because it is my nature."

I shuddered at the thought of how many scorpions I had let onto my back in the past. I loved the entire symbology of this figurine. Not only would it remind me to forego the scorpions, but it would also remind me of my duty as a mother to get my two little frogs, my son and daughter, safely to the other side of the river. This tiny statue seemed to be just one more reminder that my family tree would stop at two children, rather than the three I had always hoped for. As the sales clerk wrapped my package in tissue I felt bittersweet gratitude for the lessons frog had given me.

That afternoon when I got home I unwrapped my treasure to show Brian what I had purchased. As I told him the fable of scorpion and frog, he began turning the tiny figurine over in his hands. As he did, a small piece of clear tape on the underbelly of the frog came off, and with this the figurine opened in half. I was stunned. "Look it opens up and there is one more little frog right here in its belly," Brian remarked innocently. My eyebrows shot up in total surprise. My breath caught as I looked down at the third tiny frog which now rested in Brian's large hand. Unbeknownst to either of us right then, we had conceived a child a few days earlier. Our son was born just a few months shy of my 40th birthday. Not only did I get my third frog, I also married my prince!

• • •

I urged Don to begin thinking about the different symbolic messengers he had in his world. I am convinced that once we imbue something with meaning, it then becomes one of our messengers. If frog had not been a symbol infused with such meaning in my life, I would have missed the beautiful omen that

Brian and I received before we even knew our life had been blessed with a child.

Don laughed and asked if a washing machine could be one of the things we "infuse with meaning?" I eyed him warily, unsure if he was serious or if I was about to be the victim of another Don Borwhat zinger. He then recounted the following occurrence that had happened to him mid-week.

All Washed Up

Since Margaret's death, Don had been forced to hone his domestic abilities. Although he was no Martha Stewart, he did have a well orchestrated routine that kept him on track with all of the house chores that needed to be done. Each day of the week had its domestic task that Don would dutifully perform.

Thursdays were his least favorite. This was laundry day, and although Don never had more than a load or two of clothing to wash, he really disliked taking time away from his usual productivity to accomplish this task. On this particular Thursday he muttered some woeful self talk as he threw a load of clothes into the shiny white washer. He closed the lid and with a flip of his wrist he turned the dial and waited for the telltale rush of water that signaled that his task has begun.

But there was no rush of water, no hum of the motor... nothing. Well, this immediately added to the disdain that always bubbled just under the surface when Don had to do laundry. This was just, "freakin' beautiful," he thought. Not only did he have to waste part of his day doing laundry, but now he had to waste more of his day trying to fix the washer.

He hastily pulled the machine away from the wall to check its connections. Everything looked fine. He then headed out to the garage and checked the fuse box. Nothing amiss there either. He returned to the laundry room and fiddled with the dials once again, all to no avail. Finally before heading to find the phonebook to call a repairman he gave the washer a kick. It just sat in front of him in silent defiance.

As he thumbed through the phone book his irritation grew exponentially as he remembered the slick salesman who had talked Margaret into buying what Don had sarcastically referred to as the "Rolls Royce of washing machines" in the first place. At least the warranty would still be in effect he thought.

He dialed the number for repair and as the receptionist began to question him, he engaged himself in her conversation. To her question he responded, "No the dryer is fine; it's the washing machine that is broken." As he spoke the words, the familiar click of the washing machine beginning its first cycle filled the kitchen. The load of clothes was not the only thing that began to spin. As Don hung up the phone his mind began whirling with the following memory.

GENTLE CYCLE

In the early 70s in Margaret and Don's hometown, a frightening incident occurred that involved a young mother being held captive in her home by a fugitive. The woman's husband had phoned home during the ordeal and although he had shared a conversation with his wife, she had been unable to find a way to alert him that she was being held hostage. By the time her plight was realized the outcome had taken a tragic turn.

Being a young stay-at-home mother herself, this tragedy deeply affected Margaret. To allay her fears, Margaret insisted that she and Don devise a plan should anything like this ever occur in their lives. She decided that they needed to come up with some sort of secret phrase that she could use to alert Don if she was ever in danger. It had to be some mundane, domestic sort of banter that would raise no suspicion.

She decided that the phrase she would use to

tell Don she was in trouble would be, "The dryer is broken." Her wide eyed seriousness made him love his young wife all the more. He agreed to this "secret phrase" and then added with a laugh, "So, if the dryer is broken we are in trouble. But if you tell me the washing machine is broken, it means everything is okay?" Margaret nodded her head seriously. She was not yet able to find humor in any of it.

As the years of their marriage wore on, these two phrases became a mainstay for them. If some hardship or difficulty had befallen them Don would ask, "Does this mean the dryer is broken?" In doing so, he was really asking, "Is this serious? Are we in trouble?"

Margaret's reply was always the same, "No Don, the washer is broken, but the dryer is fine." She was saying, "Yes, this is a rough time, but we are going to be fine."

As the washing machine finished its fill cycle and began to gently churn, Don felt his grief lifting along with any stains. Margaret's message of well being was truly washing his soul clean. The washing machine was broken but the dryer was fine.

With this story, I knew Don was really beginning to tune his ears to a different sort of dialogue than he ever had before. He squirmed in his chair at the thought of trying to explain to someone that he thought Margaret was speaking to him through household appliances. I tried to soften the absurdity of it by bringing the conversation back to the fact that this was just the type of symbolic language I had been trying to describe to him.

He listened and said bluntly, "Symbolic or not, it would have been nice if she had actually done the laundry for me."

Although Don's story was humorous, he was becoming much more literate in symbolic language. Don assured me that if he called his grown son today and said, "Chris, the washing machine is broken," Chris would laugh and know that all was well in his Dad's world.

Washing machines had become a family symbol for all of them. No different than frog to me. Is it absurd to think Margaret might try to let Don know she was okay via a message involving a washing machine? Was it absurd that a small pewter frog accurately told me that I was pregnant days before a blood test ever could? The answer to this lies with the beholder.

When we are the recipient of one of these symbolic messages from the universe, they are ours alone. When the message hits home, we know it deep in our souls. Don knew the washing machine was not just about the washing machine, and the outcome for him had been a sense of peace and connection to Margaret. He vowed to keep working on his symbolic literacy, and I promised that I would assist him.

BRICK BY BRICK

At our next coffee meeting Don was unusually quiet. When I asked if anything was wrong he just smiled and said that actually a lot was right. He explained to me how things were really starting to make sense for him, and that he felt a calmness inside that he had never had before.

I could see that Don was beginning to build his own house of truth, and I felt extremely honored to be witnessing this. For myself, I knew that living within a personal belief system rife with meaning had made my life a more peaceful and satisfying journey. I could see that the same sense of peace and satisfaction was beginning to surround Don.

He was having a hard time finding the words to describe where this sense of peace was coming from. He grew a little frustrated at his inability to put his feelings into words so I asked if I could tell him just one more story. Taking a deep breath, and settling back into his chair he threw his hands up in mock surrender and said, "Sure, shoot me one more time, Godwoman!" And so I did.

THE STORY OF FOX

When Fox came into the world he was born into a loving clan. Here in the burrow of his youth, he was fed, kept warm and dry, and nurtured by his kin. As Fox began to grow, he was told by the grandfathers that some day he would choose to leave this place where he started out, to find his own home out in the world. Fox could not imagine ever wanting to leave the warmth and comfort of his clan.

As Fox lived and grew, he learned the ways of his breed. He learned how to hunt for his food; he learned how to protect the females and younger family members; and he learned how to safely travel to the edge of the meadow to explore. Fox loved his clan, and he cherished the warmth and safety that he knew in his original home. He loved the way the burrow smelled of the dark musty earth, and he treasured the way he could peer up out of the darkness to see the sunlight peeping through the hole in the ground that marked the entry to this abode.

With time came a restlessness within, and soon there began to grow a longing in Fox's spirit, a longing to run beyond the edge of the meadow where he had lived all of his days so far. Fox was hungry to know what lay beyond the horizon, but whenever he ventured too far from the burrow, he became uncertain and always turned back to that which he knew.

Even so, each time he returned from the meadow's edge, the burrow felt more and more cramped. His legs had grown longer, and he could no longer comfortably curl up at his mother's side. Even the meal portions no longer filled his belly the way they used to. The comforts he had previously known began to give way to a restlessness that was unlike anything Fox had ever known before!

Many days and many nights passed and finally the desire to stretch himself: his legs, his belly, indeed his very soul, became bigger than the fear of the unknown. As Fox took one final look at his childhood home, he committed to memory the things about the burrow that would help him to find his own home out in the world. The two things he knew for sure were that this place of comfort smelled deeply of the musty earth, and began through a hole in the ground. Fox tucked these two small truths into his memory and began his journey.

Day in and day out Fox searched for musty earth and a hole in the ground. Not long into his journey he came upon a place that seemed to match the home of his clan. Secure in the knowing that his criteria had been met, Fox curled up for a much needed rest. He trusted that he had found his home, and felt content in his heart.

Although his slumber was not as restful as he was used to, night after night Fox stayed put. As summer came, he struggled against the harsh summer heat. He did not remember summer's heat feeling like this in the home of his ancestors. And he certainly did not recall the presence of these pesky insects, which climbed up and over him day and night. Still, it met the few criteria he remembered about his childhood home so he stayed.

As summer turned to fall, and fall to winter, Fox began to feel very exposed. He did not feel sheltered or nurtured by his home. In fact he was having a hard time even remembering what real shelter felt like. Over and over in his mind, he envisioned the mental checklist of what his home was to be like, and each time he was unable to understand why the home he has chosen did not feel quite right.

As fox spends his nights in the cold, and struggles to survive the harsh elements, he becomes disillusioned. He thinks to himself, "This home I have found, it does not shelter me as the home of my clan did. It does not offer me a safe haven from which to escape bear, nor does it allow me to lay down at night to sweet dreams of chasing dragonflies in the meadow. I live in torment, yet I have followed the ways of my clan." Fox falls deeper and deeper into despair.

It turns out that Hawk had been watching Fox for many days. As Fox's disillusionment grew, so did Hawk's compassion. Unable to stay circling far above the situation any longer, Hawk alighted in a tree near Fox. Hawk asked Fox about the source of his distress. Fox began the telling of his forlorn tale. Hawk listened quietly.

When Fox finished explaining his plight, Hawk simply shook her head. She confided that she too had once found herself in a similar situation. When she first flew free from her childhood nest, she had searched far and wide for a home that matched her perception of what home should be. She knew that her home would be made of branches, and that it would be near a river. Soon into her journey she found a place that fit, and she settled into her new life.

Before long her disillusionment began to grow. Like Fox, the home she had chosen did not feel like it offered her any of the shelter that she had known in her youth. It was not until Raccoon sauntered by to share his story, that she realized the mistake she had made. "Yes, yes, the twigs were there, and yes the river was there as well. But the house she found belonged not to her, but instead to Beaver!"

She gently explained to Fox that she had learned

that a dwelling is made, not found. She now took great joy in choosing each stick that went into the building of her nest. Indeed it was her own careful placement of each piece that had truly made it her home. Fox was thoughtful for a long time, his deep reverie broken only by the occasional twitching of his tail, as he whisked an errant bug from his coat.

With a sly grin Hawk could keep her silence no longer. "Excuse me Fox," she said, "Can you please move a bit to the side?" Fox slowly raised himself up from the spot he had lain upon for so long. He looked at Hawk with bewilderment. She never took her eyes from his as she gently replied. "My fledglings are hungry and waiting back at the nest. If you will kindly remove yourself from atop this ant-hill I will bring some of these red juicy ants to my babies."

With a flap of her wings, she was gone and Fox was left suddenly alone with the truth: he had mistaken an anthill for his own home. His mind reeled...the smell of musty earth, the hole in the ground. He had focused so intently upon what he "knew" about the home of his past, that it had rendered him unable to see his own path. He could now see that, like Hawk, he had tried to make the home of another into his own. With this newfound wisdom, Fox's journey began in earnest that day. Before long Fox had used his own paws to create the burrow that he now called home.

It was many days and many nights later that Fox came upon Spider. Spider was noticeably distressed as she struggled to get comfortable in the misshapen puff of a dandelion flower. Fox smiled to himself, supposing that Spider had started off some time ago looking for a place that was silvery and soft, like the web of her youth. Fox knew it was time to share his story, just as Hawk had shared hers. He settled down next to Spider, and began the telling of his tale.

• • •

When Don had said, "Shoot me," I guess my aim was true because he clearly got the story just as I had intended it. "So you are Hawk and I am Fox! You have been circling above watching me look for my own home, and with your gentle prodding and stories you have helped to open my eyes. And maybe someday it will be my turn to help someone like spider, not by telling them what the truth is, but by holding the door open while they search on their own?" I broke into a huge grin and simply nodded my head. I knew inside that Don's agreement to share his white rock story would indeed hold that door open for many.

Although I'm sure that business continued as usual at the coffee shop, for Don and I time stood still. Like the steam rising up from the white mugs that sat on the table before us, we both felt ourselves being lifted, and this time we were lifted without words or stories. It was the holy silence between us that was speaking volumes. A deep sense of satisfaction washed over me, and I really felt like my friend Don, the skeptical businessman who rued the day that the word foo foo had become part of his vocabulary, had somehow found shelter in his own house of truth.

PART FOUR

HALFWAY ACROSS THE RIVER

If I follow the origins of this book backwards, it was the story of the stone Madonna in Carmel that moved Margaret so deeply that she decided to force a "play date" between Don and I. In doing so it was her hope that together we could find a way to share these kinds of stories with others. Margaret was always one to succeed at what she had set her mind to, and even from the other side she seemed well equipped to carry out her goal.

Throughout the writing of this book, extraordinary phenomena continued to happen to both Don and I. Many days would find us on the phone together recounting small events that hinted at Margaret's continued involvement in our work. One night, late in the writing process, as I re-read my words, I remarked to my husband that I was thinking that what I had written that day was nearly the last chapter of the book. As my eyes consumed the very last sentence on the very last page, the light above our bed turned off. My husband, being well accustomed to otherworld happenings in our home simply asked, "So what is Margaret telling you?" I just smiled and said, "I guess it's lights out for the book. I will wrap it up with a closing chapter tomorrow. I think Margaret is letting me know it is done. The only thing I have left to do is come up with a title."

At that, I closed my eyes and drifted into a deep and peaceful sleep. That night I dreamt of Margaret, and of a conversation we had shared while she was alive. This exchange occurred on a day when Margaret was feeling particularly pensive about how her future was going to unfold. She stood staring out the window, carefully measuring her words before she spoke.

"Annette I want to be prepared. How will I know when death is near me?" The words hung heavy in the air between us. As she turned to face me, it seemed that an unseen hand had suddenly swept the morning mist from my eyes; at that moment I saw clearly that my friend was dying. After this it was one of those conversations that came through me, but not from me. I answered her gently, with a serenity that belied my sadness.

"Margaret, you're halfway across the river asking me what it is going to be like when the water hits you. You are *in* the water Margaret, and one day you will have crossed the entire river and then you will find yourself on the other side."

Both Margaret and I were deeply moved by my words. She immediately knew that what I had spoken was a truth of the highest order. She smiled and affirmed out loud that yes, she truly was right in the middle of the river, in essence right in the middle of dying, and dying was not nearly as bad as she had always feared it would be. She said to me that day, and many times afterwards, that if there was one message she could pass on to others, it would be that living through the terminal stages of a disease was simply not as hard as she had always feared it would be. She had wanted to make a DVD together showing her in the last stages of her life living this very message. Our plans were to show conversations about death and dying between Margaret and me. We figured that the visual honesty of a dying woman talking peacefully about her own death was going to be very healing to anyone who feared the very place Margaret was in.

Our DVD was to be named, "Halfway Across the River," in honor of our sacred conversation that day. Margaret was very excited about the project. She really felt that she might be able to allay the fear of the dying process for others, a fear she felt she had needlessly expended energy on in her own life. Although Margaret was "terminal" for many months, her actual physical decline occurred in a matter of days, leaving the plans for our visual message undone, and her goal unmet.

Margaret was not the type to leave things undone, and it appeared that she had no intention of letting this last endeavor go either. She always did have a lively and impish sense of humor, and in my final night-time visit from her, she was no different. In the dream, after recounting our profound conversation about the river, she smiled and said that time had been short all along, and that I, of all people should have seen the sign.

"What sign?" I asked.

With a smile on her face and a glimmer in her eye she said simply, "The street sign where I lived, Annette."

Don and Margaret had made their home on a street called *Swiftwater Court.** I awoke with the misty memory of Margaret in dreamtime hovering around me like a soft blanket. The symbology of that sign, it was uncanny. The day we had talked so eloquently about her journey across the river, we didn't know that she was in swift water, that the current was

---

* the street name has been altered slightly to protect Don's privacy.

moving quite so fast. Even so, I knew in my heart that Margaret truly had reached the other side, and she was simply sending a message of encouragement for the rest of us who were still just halfway across.

AFTERWORD

AFTERWORD

I suppose that events like those recounted in this book might seem extraordinary to some. Yet in my life, occurrences such as these have become a welcome and routine part of my daily reality. Every story in this book is true. At times names and details have been altered to protect confidentiality, but each experience unfolded just the way I have recounted it.

We can never underestimate the power of a story... mine, yours, anyones. Stories move us at a deep level, reminding us of the greatness that is apparent not just within ourselves, but in our fellow human beings as well. I consider myself to be a sacred storyteller, one who has been entrusted with the stories of some very great souls and it has been my great pleasure to put their stories into print.

As far as my personal house of truth goes, it is pretty simple. I feel like I have been taught by the dying how to walk the path of an everyday mystic, a regular person who finds a way to commune with a source that gives guidance, meaning, and direction to my everyday life. I am fortunate to live in a time when science regularly corroborates the fact that matter and energy are far more fluid than we once ever imagined. What the Ancients supposed, science is now validating.

The synchronicities, the small miracles, even the beautiful, eloquent communication I shared with the universe that day in Carmel is a dialogue that I believe is available to each of us, and I think it has been my close work with the dying that has taught me how to live with one foot in each world. The dying have certainly been my teachers in how to see the world through eyes of wonder.

As Don and I shared our coffee time conversations, it became clear to him that those close to death really do seem able to live with one foot in each world. At the beginning of our talks Don often wondered, "Why is it that we wait until our days have grown short to open up?" Before long he began to understand the irony of this question in his own life; for he knew if it had not been for the manifestation of the white rock on his pillow in New York, he would never have willingly engaged in any of our conversations together. A light bulb went on for him; it was not just the dying who could open up earlier…it was all of us.

Don was aware that not everyone gets a white rock left on their pillow, and he wondered how it was that we could help people crack open that doorway to their own house of truth. Don knew he could not give people his white rock, just as he could not hand them his house of truth. What he could do was share his story with others. It is not a small thing to ask a man who has spent his life receiving acclaim from a hard nosed business world to expose this white rock tale.

Thankfully, there is enough renegade in Don that he shrugged off the potential embarrassment he might face with his peers, and agreed to allow me to share his tale. He further justified his public unveiling by lamenting over the fact that he was terrified of the "cosmic kick in the a - -" he would get from Margaret if he didn't do this foo foo stuff with me.

Foo foo aside, I believe we all at some point get our white rock. What we choose to do with it is what decides our path. Hopefully the stories in this book have not only reminded you of the white rocks that have shown themselves in your world, but also primed your vision to see the many that still lay on the pathway before you.

Afterword 2.0

Lest I leave any readers with the incorrect assumption that Don Borwhat has gone soft with the publication of this book, I thought it best to include the actual e-mail he sent me after I had forwarded him the pages which marked the ending of the book. As I waited anxiously for what I was sure was going to be a heartfelt reply from him, this is what actually arrived:

> *The ending was moving. What ends for us*
> *at the coffee shop is what I hope is a begin-*
> *ning of a new journey for others. We should*
> *give everyone a gift certificate to Starbucks*
> *to start them on their journey. I used to be*
> *such a normal guy until I got hooked up*
> *with you...now you have me all f----d up.*
> *Don*

A truly irreverent way to end a book about the "foo foo" stuff of life, but if I sugar coated it, well it simply would not be Don.

Don's only request of me, in exchange for the public unveiling of the white rock story, was to use a portion of the proceeds from this book to further the cancer advocacy work that was such a part of Margaret's legacy. To learn more about this, or to donate directly to the cause, please go to the Margaret's House page on my website at www.onecandle.net.

This arrangement feeds Don's unrelenting need to exercise his razor sharp business skills while still accomplishing his newfound goal of "giving back," allowing him to essentially kill two birds with one (heart shaped) stone.

THE LAST WORD
BY DON BORWHAT

THE LAST WORD

As much as it horrifies me to be putting my two cents worth into a foo foo book like this, I really see no choice in the matter. Also, having the last word is kind of nice.

Years ago when Margaret first introduced me to the Godwoman, I truly thought she was an unusual combination of strange and stupid. Trust me, at the beginning not only did I not want to have a friendship with her, I did not even want to be in the same room with her. The foo foo stuff she and Margaret talked about was all hocus pocus to me and I wanted no part of any of it. It worked for them and that is where I believed it should stay.

As Margaret's friendship with the Godwoman became stronger, and I got to know Annette better, my viewpoint changed. The Godwoman was definitely not stupid, and her strange ways offered Margaret a type of healing that moved even cynical me. When Margaret met the Godwoman, she was afraid of dying. The Godwoman and her stories really did change this. Margaret's fear began to fade and was replaced with a serenity that carried through to her last day.

Before Margaret died she let me know two things very clearly. The first was that she wanted me to continue on with her work in cancer advocacy, and the second was that she wanted me to help the Godwoman get her stories out to others, so they could know the same comfort from Annette's work as she had. I figured I could cover the cancer advocacy part by continuing my work with WCAN (the non-profit Margaret started years ago), but the second part of helping the Godwoman on her mission to share foo foo with the world? Damn! Did this really have to be the last wish of my dying wife? Little did I know at the time that the Godwoman was going to be indispensable to me as I tried to adjust my worldview to the truly unexplainable events that surround that white heart-shaped rock.

The white heart-shaped rock... this was and still is a great puzzle to me. It is an event that changed my relationship with reality. Of course, events like the white rock are all in a day's work to the Godwoman, but for a cynic like me, this is devastating stuff! I can tell you from experience, that the "unbelievable" things that Annette writes about . . . well they may be unbelievable, but they are also true. If there is another world awaiting us (and now I am pretty sure there might be) the Godwoman definitely has one foot there already.

I gave Annette permission to tell my story not because I want to prove anything. I don't. I did not share this story because I am hoping for financial gain. I make a great living and I simply don't need it. In fact I have requested, and have made it very clear, that I want no financial ties to the book at all. In response to my request, the Godwoman is donating a portion of the proceeds from each book to WCAN, which I really appreciate. In allowing Annette to share this story, my hope is simple. That it might help others. If my story brings peace to those who are grieving, if it brings comfort to those who are facing death, then I have done my job.

Margaret was an incredible woman, and Annette has done a great job capturing her spirit in this book. As much as I hate to admit it, the Godwoman is a pretty incredible woman as well. Margaret believed that she had a gift that the world needed. I agree.

I guess in retrospect, I do understand why my dying wife would saddle me with the last request of helping the Godwoman get her message out to the world. It is simply the right thing to do.

I think by sharing my story I have fulfilled my wife's last request. In honor of Margaret and in honor of the Godwoman, I hope this book soars. If this happens, I shudder at the thought of my business colleagues finding out about my dark "Godwoman" secret. They will no doubt wonder what the hell happened to me, and why I would go public with such a foo foo story. Again, the reason is simple: it's the right thing to do. For fifteen years after her cancer diagnosis, I watched Margaret put helping others as number one on her agenda. Following in her footsteps by doing the right thing with this story was easy.

And for any of you foo foo people who think you want to contact me to give me some well meaning piece of new age advice, save it for the Godwoman. I'm busy back in the world of business.

Sincerely,
Don Borwhat

RESOURCES

ANNETTE'S BOOKSHELF

These are just a few of the books that have taught me and touched me.

Sacred Dying. by Megory Anderson,
   Marlowe & Company, 2003

Testimony of Light. Helen Greaves
   Rider; New Ed edition 2005

Final Gifts. Maggie Callanan and Patricia Kelley
   Bantam; 1997

The Four Things that Matter Most. Ira Byock, M.D.
   Free Press; 2004

**Afterlife Encounters: Ordinary People
Extraordinary Experiences.** Dianne Arcangel, M.S.
   Hampton Roads Publishing, 2005

Subtle Energy. William Collinge, Ph.D.
   Warner Books, Inc., 1998

Healing Words. Larry Dossey, M.D.
HarperCollins Publishers, 1993

Healing Through Prayer. Larry Dossey and Others
Anglican Book Centre, 1999

The Power of Kindness. Piero Ferrucci, Jeremy P. Tarcher
Penguin, 2006

The Healing Power of Sound. Mitchell L. Gaynor, M.D.
Shambhala Publications, Inc., 2006

Where Two Worlds Touch. Gloria D. Karpinski
Ballantine Books, 1990

Limitless Mind. Jane Katra, Ph.D. and Russell Targ
New World Library; 1999

The Heart of the Mind. Jane Katra, Ph.D., and Russell Targ
New World Library, 1999

Everything Happens for a Reason. Mira Kirshenbaum
Harmony Books, 2004

Life After Loss. Raymond Moody, Jr., M.D. Ph.D.,
and Dianne Arcangel, M.S.
HarperCollins Publishers, Inc., 2001

Dark Nights of the Soul. Thomas Moore
Gotham Books, 2004

The Biology of Transcendence. Joseph Chilton Pearce
Park Street Press, 2002

Heading Toward Omega. Kenneth Ring
William Morrow and Company, Inc., 1985

Lessons from the Light. Kenneth Ring,
and Evelyn Elsaesser Valarino
Insight Books, 1998

Elegant Choices, Healing Choices. Marsha Sinetar
Paulist Press, 1988

Ordinary People as Monks and Mystics. Marsha Sinetar
Paulist Press, 1986

Many Lives, Many Masters. Brian Weiss, M.D.
Simon & Schuster, 1988.

MARGARET'S BOOKSHELF

These are books that Margaret asked Don to give to me after her death. Although we never spoke about these titles, I am certain she left them to me with reason, so I have included them here.

Getting Doctors to Listen. Philip J., Boyle, ed.
Georgetown University Press, 2000

Dying Well. Ira Byock, M.D.
Riverhead Books, 1997

The Myth of Women's Masochism. Paula J. Caplan, Ph.D.
E.P. Dutton, 1985

The Needs of the Dying. David Kessler
HarperCollins Publishers, 1997

On Death and Dying. Elisabeth Kubler-Ross
Macmillan Publishing Co., 1969

What Dying People Want. David Kuhl, M.D.
New York: PublicAffairs, 2002

Facing Death and Finding Hope. Christine Longaker
Broadway Books, 1997

Our Greatest Gift. Henri J.M. Nouwen
  HarperCollins Publishers, 1994

The Grace in Dying. Kathleen Dowling Singh
  HarperCollins Publishers, 1998

The Journey Beyond Breast Cancer.
  Virginia M. Rochester Soffa,
  Healing Arts Press, 1994

A Few Months to Live. Jana Staton, Roger Shuy, and Ira Byock
  Georgetown University Press, 2001

Organizations

The International Association for Near Death Studies, Inc.
P.O. Box 502 East Windsor Hill, CT 06028
Tel: 806.882.1211
www.iands.org

The Institute of Noetic Sciences
101 San Antonio Road, Petaluma, CA 94952, USA
Tel: 707-775-3500
www.ions.org

DVDs

What the Bleep Do we Know?
Twentieth Century Fox
www.whatthebleep.com

Spiritual Cinema Circle
www.spiritualcinemacircle.com

WEBSITES

Foreverfamilyfoundation.org
A public service site that offers links, newsletters and information on afterlife sciences

Veritas.arizona.edu
A university site which houses original research, reading materials, and links pertaining to afterlife sciences.

For ordering information
or to correspond
with the author please contact

One Candle, LLC

at

Dr. Childs is available for private consultations,
workshops and lectures.
For more information on her work, or to schedule an event,
Please visit the One Candle website or call:

1-866-819-4133

To contact Don Borwhat
or to learn more about
The Women's Cancer Advocacy Network
and Margaret's House
Please contact
www.WCAN.org

1-877-984-WCAN

or visit the "Margaret's House" page at
www.onecandle.net

Further acclaim for
Annette Childs and
Will You Dance...

"This tiny treasure is a bringer of light, illuminating that which is true and yet can seem so illusive in times of darkness. Each page is like a heart filled gift of poetry and art. Annette Childs shines an uncommon wisdom and light into this world."

Rebecca Tolin
KPBS Broadcasting
San Diego

"This book of perennial wisdom is positioned somewhere between heaven and earth. Written by a wisdom teacher, teaching us how our own wounding deepens our vision and renders us wiser. In this book, Annette Childs offers Hope Faith and Joy, if only you will take her hand and Dance!"

Linda Whitney Peterson, Ph.D.
Director of Behavioral Sciences University of Nevada
School of Medicine, Department of Family Medicine

" A statement of eternal truth, clearly and gently challenging us to honor those pivotal moments of our own lives when we can recognize and risk living our life purpose."

Dennis Holz, Founder
Source Seminars

"Dr. Annette Childs has written a story which will lend hope and strength to many who are facing times of darkness. A fable in the old tradition—lyrical, intuitively wrought, with a simple but profound message—will you dance? And the question, leads us into this tale of Destiny's impact in our lives, and how will we cope with inevitable change. We recognize how moments which come unbidden into our lives can be moments of great challenge, great courage, and great potential transformation."

Michael S. Hutton, Ph.D., MFT
Core Faculty Institute of Transpersonal Psychology

About the Author

ANNETTE CHILDS holds a Ph.D. in psychology and maintains a private practice assisting individuals and families to grow through painful transitions. She has devoted much of her work to assisting the dying and their families to find peace and meaning at the end of life.

As a researcher she has extensively studied the near death experience and other mystical phenomenon, and has contributed original research to the field of near death studies.

A self-taught wordsmith who writes from the heart, her style is rich with metaphor and symbolism. Her first book, *Will You Dance?*, received critical acclaim and was the recipient of three national awards including, New Age Book of the Year, and the Benjamin Franklin Award.

She lives in the Western United States with her husband Brian and three children.

For more information on her work,
please visit *www.onecandle.net*